D1588157

RARY

LEGE OF RIPON

Coll. of Ripon & York St John

3 8025 00145202 1

RYSJ

The Ernest Press
© Tony Wimbush 1987

Book design, maps and sketches by the author

Front cover: Lilla Cross by Mike Williams

Wimbush, Tony
    Moorland Challenge : A long distance
walker's guide to the North York Moors,
the Wolds and adjacent areas.
1. England, Northern – Description and
travel – Guide-books
I. Title
914.28'04858   DA670. N813

ISBN 0-948153-04-0

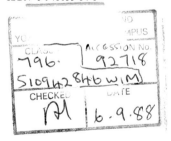

NOTE

Whilst every care has been taken by the author in compiling this book all the routes outlined are undertaken at the individual's own risk. Neither the author nor the publisher can accept any responsibility whatsoever for any consequences arising out of the use of this book. The inclusion of a route should not be taken as implying a legal right of way or access.

All address and publications given in this book were current at the time of going to press but it is inevitable that addresses or availability of publications may change. Neither the author nor the publisher can accept responsibility for the inconvenience this may cause the reader.

MOORLAND CHALLENGE

by
TONY WIMBUSH

COLLEGE OF RIPON
AND YORK ST JOHN
YORK CAMPUS
LIBRARY

A long distance walker's guide to the North York Moors, the Wolds and adjacent areas

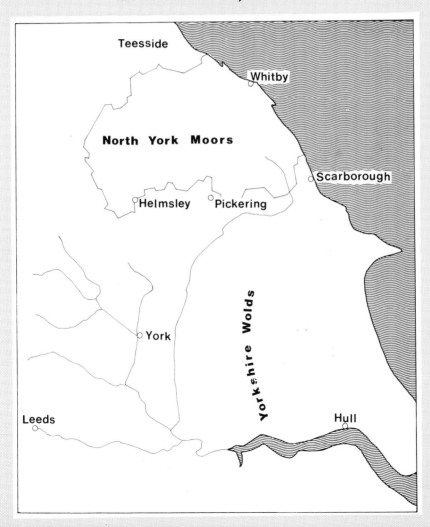

CONTENTS

PREFACE

"There is no orthodoxy in walking, it is a land of many paths and no paths where everyone goes his own way and is right."

G. M. Trevelyan

Long distance challenges appear to be virtually inexhaustible with new routes being promoted every year. Like fell running, orienteering and Munro-bagging, long distance walking has become a distinct branch of the outdoor scene with is own dedicated following of enthusiasts. No doubt the Lyke Wake Walk and the Pennine Way have generated much of the interest that has paved the way for many of these walks, most of which offer attractive badges for their successful completion. One of the main reasons for this is that they capture the best of both the worlds of sport and recreation. The drive and discipline of sport are shared with the freedom and informality of recreation. This allows everyone to participate at their own level of fitness and ability. Whether you are a casual walker or a trained athlete you can still enjoy the same sense of achievement and satisfaction, and in this respect everyone can be a winner.

Another of the great virtues of long distance walking is that so much can be brought together and contrasted within the compass of a single day. Some may say there is little time to stand and stare. But what better way to comprehend the immense beauty of an area than on foot striding across the landscape: to traverse the moorland tops, to climb the dividing ridges and to saunter along the dales, to go on and on from dawn to dusk, to know the natural world in all its changing seasons and all its subtle interplay of light, form, colour and texture. No, nothing can cultivate an eye for the beauty of the landscape so well as the practice of measuring it with your own legs. Then there are the other rewards: the exaltation of a good day out on the moors when mind and body merge into an effortless rhythm with the surrounding world and all is in tune; the spirit of the eternal hills and the friendships that it engenders; and not least the memories and experiences that will last a lifetime.

TONY WIMBUSH
December 1986

INTRODUCTION

While there are many books for today's walker few deal exclusively with the more adventurous and challenging aspects of walking. This guide brings under one cover the enormous variety of walks which now traverse the North York Moors, the Wolds and adjacent areas. Generally only routes of twenty miles or more are considered to qualify as long distance. Here this definition has been extended slightly to include any walk where a badge is issued together with named recreational paths of ten miles or more. Clearly it is beyond the scope of any one guide to give detailed descriptions of all the routes indicated. The main purpose throughout has been to provide an overall picture of the walks which exist together with further sources of information, particularly for some of the lesser known walks which are published by voluntary, rather than commercial, organisations. The routes have been arranged into three main categories.

Challenges These are walks which can be completed at any time and for which badges are awarded. Few of the walks have time limits but it has become general practice to complete them in either a continuous attempt or on consecutive days. Of the fifteen routes outlined only three have commercially produced guides, the remainder are covered by a variety of route sheets and leaflets available from their respective walk secretaries. In all cases the maps and route guides included here should prove to be an invaluable supplement.

Events These are organised annually on specific dates each year and have to be entered in advance by application to the entry secretaries shown. In most cases walkers are left to devise their own route between a list of checkpoints. For organisational reasons a time limit is imposed for completing the route and badges are available to all successful participants.

Paths This section provides an information directory to all the long distance paths in the area. They can be completed on consecutive days, in random sections or where practical in a day's outing. As some of the route guides are only available locally it is hoped the directory will help promote some of the lesser known and least frequented paths.

Finally, scattered throughout the pages that follow are a number of photographs and quotations which have been selected to illustrate the character, the people and the places associated with this unique region. Like a good picture a good quotation is worth a thousand words; it somehow captures the truth and essence of its subject in a few succinct lines. Those included here have been selected mostly from material which is now out-of-print. Yet many of these passages have a quality and freshness that is not often found in modern writing. It is hoped they will help bring interest, colour and perspective into a scene where they might otherwise be lacking.

CHALLENGES

Walks which can be completed at any time and for which badges and certificates are awarded

Wainstones

ANYTIME CHALLENGE WALKS

WALK	AREA	MILEAGE
Beverley '20'	Wolds	20
Bilsdale Circuit	Moors	29
East Thridings Treble Ten	Wolds	29
Hambleton Hobble	Moors	30
High Hunsley Circuit	Wolds	24½
Humber Bridge Link	Wolds	34
Lyke Wake Walk	Moors	40
North Wolds Walk	Wolds	20
Rosedale Circuit	Moors	37
Samaritan Way	Moors	38
Scarborough Rock	Moors	26
Scarborough Samaritans Challenge	Moors	26
Seahorse Saunter	Moors	43
Shepherd's Round	Moors	36
White Rose Walk	Moors	37,34,31

Others:

Monks Trod	Moors	20
Rail Trail	Moors	20
Three Feathers Walk	Moors	30
Hutton Hike	Wolds	23
Rudston Roam	Wolds	23
Headland Walk	Coast	20
J.M. Moors Challenge	Moors	24

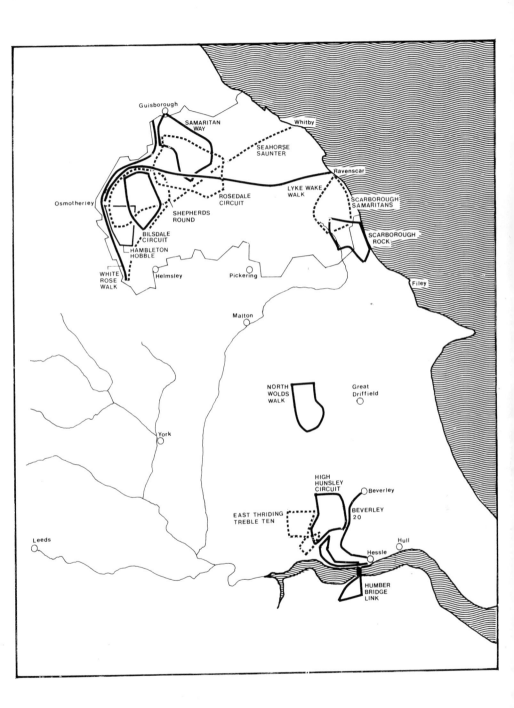

CHALLENGES

- Can be attempted at any time

- Specific route and distance to be completed

- Route description, certificates and badges are issued by a walk secretary

- Route usually has to be completed as a continuous exercise, sometimes within a time limit

- Navigational ability essential

- Essentially a sporting challenge

- Walkers are not generally sponsored

- While all information was up-to-date at the time of publication the addresses of walk secretaries can change or walks can be discontinued

- A standard format has been used in displaying information in this section as shown below.

BEVERLEY '20'		wolds		20 miles × 500 feet	
name		*area*		*distance*	*ascent*

Hessle	033 255	Beverley	038 393	12 hours limit
start	*grid ref*	*finish*	*grid ref*	*maximum time allowed*

O S SHEET 106 – 1: 50 000
map   *scale*

GLEN HOOD, 329 KINGTSON ROAD, WILLERBY, HULL HU10 6PY (S.A.E.)
Name and address from which a route description and details of the badge and certificate can be obtained. ALWAYS ENCLOSE A STAMPED ADDRESSED ENVELOPE.

BEVERLEY '20' RECREATIONAL FOOTPATH LEAFLET, HUMBERSIDE COUNTY COUNCIL
Name of publication author and publisher (where applicable).

ROUTE GUIDE – *key points on the route together with a 2½ mph route schedule. This can be adapted to your intended start time to compile a personal route schedule. Arrival times can then be noted to monitor progress and provide a permanent record.*

TEXT
Origin – description – characteristics – difficulty – etc.

◀ Lilla Cross

| BEVERLEY '20' | Wolds | 20 miles × 500 feet |

Hessle 033 255 Beverley 038 393 12 hours limit
O S Sheet 106 – 1: 50 000
Glen Hood, 329 Kingston Road, Willerby, Hull, Humberside HU10 6PY (SAE)
Beverley '20' Recreational Footpath Leaflet, Humberside County Council
Route Guide

No	Grid Ref	Location	Distance miles	2½ mph pace
1	033 255	Hessle	0	0
2	983 251	Long Plantation	4	135
3	970 291	Welton Wold Farm	8	3-12
4	975 311	York Ground Farm	9½	3-50
5	015 338	Skidby	13	5-10
6	020 360	Bentley	15	6-00
7	038 393	Beverley Minster	20	8-00

The Beverley '20' was the first challenge walk to be promoted in the Wolds as well as forming the first section of the East Riding Heritage Way which stretches some 84 miles from the Humber Bridge to Filey (see pages 73 and 74). The area has since become immensely popular with several other challenges following in its wake. Glen Hood pioneered the walk in 1979 in conjunction with Humberside County Council; it stands as an excellent example of what can be achieved by the successful partnership of the voluntary and public sectors of the community. The route has been waymarked in both directions and offers several alternatives all of which are fully described in the leaflet published by Humberside C.C. and available from Glen Hood together with information on the badge. That indefatigable tramper, A.J. Brown once commented that the people of Hull had far better sea-legs than land-legs and preferred to cycle when they could not sail. He would certainly have no cause for complaint today!

It does not so much matter which way you go to Beverley, as long as you do go, for Beverley is one of the jewels of the East Riding. For a capital town it is surprisingly small, but that is one of its charms. There is a long mainstreet, a few side streets, a glorious market square, a generous sprinkling of inns, an old bar and two noble churches.

A.J. Brown
Striding Through Yorkshire, 1938

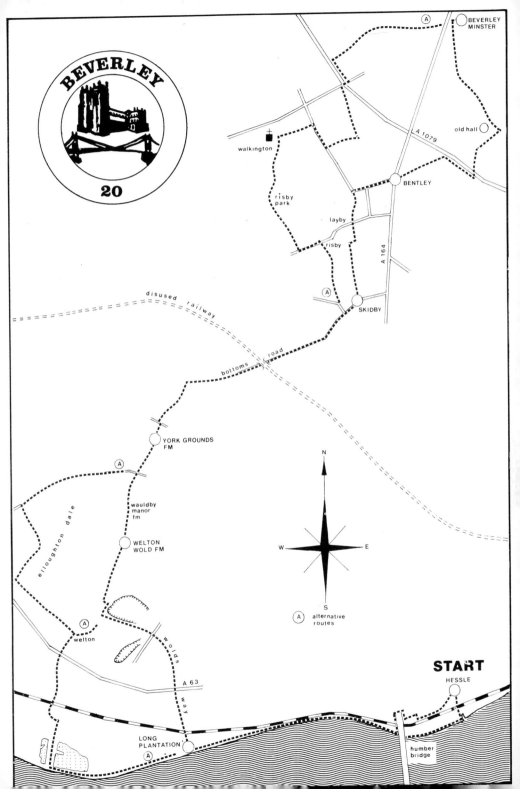

BILSDALE CIRCUIT　　　Moors　　　29 miles × 4000 feet

Newgate Car Park 564 890 Circular No time limit
Nork York Moors Outdoor Leisure Map – West 1: 25 000
Mike Teanby, Old School House, Village Stret, Adwick le Street, Doncaster, DN6 7AD, South Yorkshire
The Bilsdale Circuit, Michael Teanby, Dalesman 1981
Route Guide

No	Grid Ref	Location	Distance miles	2½ mph pace
1	564 890	Newgate Bank	0	0
2	539 917	Moorgate	4	1-40
3	545 948	High Thwaites	6	2-25
4	523 030	Carlton Bank	12	4-50
5	513 033	Hasty Bank	16	6-25
6	582 988	Tripsdale Beck	20	8-00
7	610 964	Bilsdale Bridleway	22	8-50
8	603 923	Bogmire Gill	25	10-00
9	564 890	Newgate Bank	29	11-35

Mike Teanby inaugurated this route in 1977 on behalf of the North Yorkshire Long Distance Walkers' Association. Since that time it has become a popular alternative to the Lyke Wake as well as appearing on the challenge event calendar on a number of occasions. The Bilsdale has all the ingredients of a good moorland walk – fine views, steep ascents and a good measure of rough terrain all make the circuit a demanding but rewarding objective.

> There is no better lounging place than a moor. It is a kind of clean bare antechamber to Heaven. There is a subtle variety in its slowly changing patterns of cloud and shadow and tinted horizons, sufficient to keep up a flicker of interest in the mind all day. With its velvet patches, no bigger than a drawing room carpet, of fine moorland grass, its surfaces invite repose. Its remoteness, its permanence, its old and sprawling indifference to man and his concerns, rest and cleanse the mind. All the noises of the world are drowned in the one monotonous cry of the curlew.
>
> J.B. Priestley

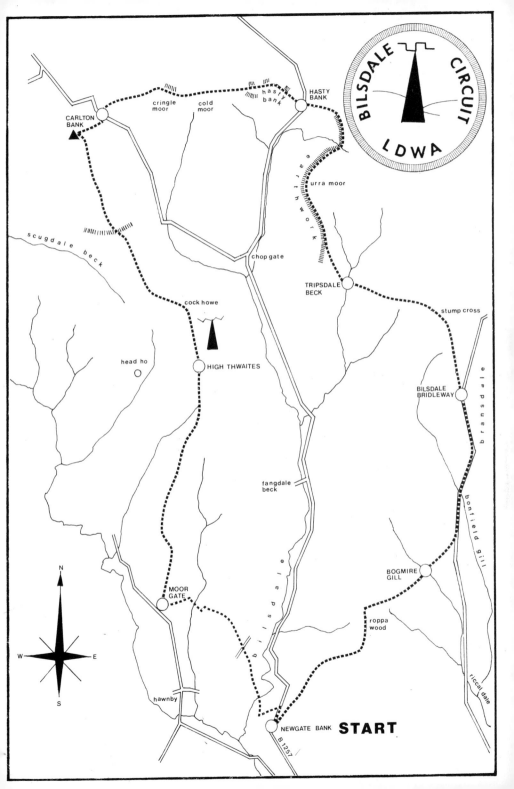

EAST THRIDINGS TREBLE TEN Wolds 29 miles × 750 feet

Welton Church 959 272 Circular No time limit

O S Sheet 106 – 1: 50 000

Kim Peacock, 16 Denesway, Swanland Road, Hessle, Humberside
HU13 0NL (SAE)

Route Guide

No	Grid Ref	Location	Distance miles	2½ mph pace
1	959 272	Welton Church	0	0
2	986 295	Little Wauldby Farm	3	1-10
3	948 298	Spout Hill	6	2-25
4	926 313	South Cave	9	3-35
5	939 349	High Hunsley Road	12	4-50
6	897 327	North Cave Church	16	6-25
7	880 311	A63	18	7-20
8	903 297	Mill Beck	20	8-00
9	940 294	Brantingham	23	9-10
10	964 288	Welton Road	26	10-25
11	959 272	Welton Church	28	11-12

Conceived in the late 1960's by Kim Peacock this route eventually came into being
in 1981. The walk starts and finishes at Welton, famous for the Green Dragon Inn
which was one of the favourite haunts of highwayman Dick Turpin before he was
captured and hanged at York. The figure-of-eight route winds its way round the
rolling South Wolds country west of Hull taking in many of its delightful villages
and dry dales. There are no restrictions on how the walk should be done and many
walkers take two or three days.

It was common among the Norsemen of old to divide lands
into three portions for the purposes of government, and their
name for each portion was thrithjungr. This mysterious word
means in our tongue "a third part" and from it arose the
English word Thridings as companion to feorthing, another
word which we use today in a very slightly altered form. But
the difficulty of pronouncing distinctly and easily the
combination "North Thriding" is evident, and the troublesome
word suffered the same fate as commonly then befell the
troublesome man – it got, quite naturally, beheaded.

H. B. Browne
The Story of the East Riding, 1912

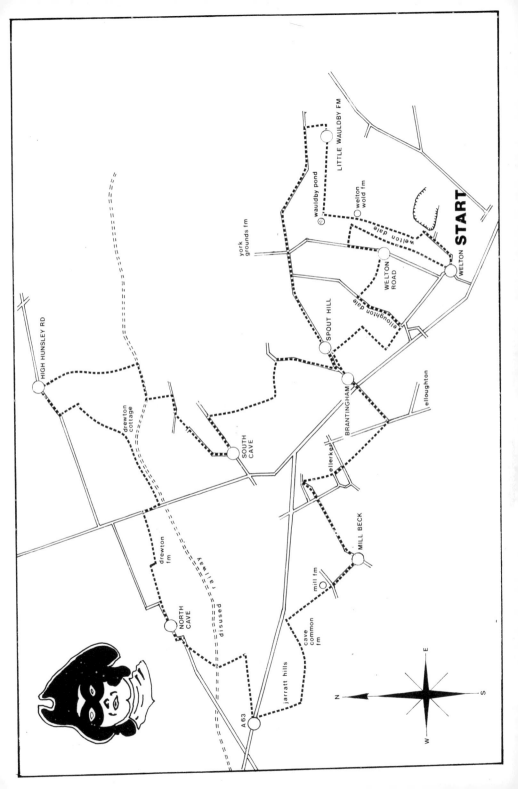

HAMBLETON HOBBLE	Moors	30 miles × 2 500 feet

Osmotherley 456 972 Circular No time limit
North York Moors Outdoor Leisure Map – West 1:25 000
P. A. Sherwood, Wits End, South Kilvington, Thirsk, North Yorkshire
YO7 2NF. (SAE)
Route Guide

No	Grid Ref	Location	Distance miles	2½ mph pace
1	456 973	Osmotherley	0	0
2	486 957	Robinson's Cross	2½	1-00
3	520 907	Arden Hall	8	3-10
4	536 880	Murton Grange	11	4-25
5	549 858	Old Byland	13	5-10
6	532 861	Wethercote Lane	17	6-50
7	500 868	Hesketh Hall	20	8-00
8	466 907	New Kepwick	24	9-35
9	451 933	Over Silton	26	10-25
10	456 973	Osmotherley	30	11-12

The Hambleton Hobble was devised by P. A. Sherwood, mace bearer of the Lyke Wake Club, to help relieve some of the pressure from the Lyke Wake Walk. The circuit connects the village pubs at Osmotherley, Hawnby, Scawton and Nether Silton following little-used field paths. While the walk is essentially a challenge the nature of the route does not facilitate speed and there is no time limit. An unsurfaced road between Arden Hall and Kepwick allows the walk to be completed in two shorter circuits of under twenty miles if desired.

It is surprising that more challenges have not been contrived to link together the village pubs which are scattered across the countryside. There is a lot to be said for a lunch-time stop at a village inn but it is in the evening after a good long walk that they really begin to weave their magic spell. The right company, the right ale and an inn that exudes a character and friendliness making it different from any other, surely that is the crowning glory of the day's pilgrimage!

> I do not say that the substitution of ale for tea as the national beverage would immediately restore the real gold standard and with it stability and prosperity throughout the land, but I do say it is high time we got rid of the false notion that the powerful tea drug is a more respectable and less harmful drink than ale.
>
> A. J. Brown
> Moorland Tramping, 1930

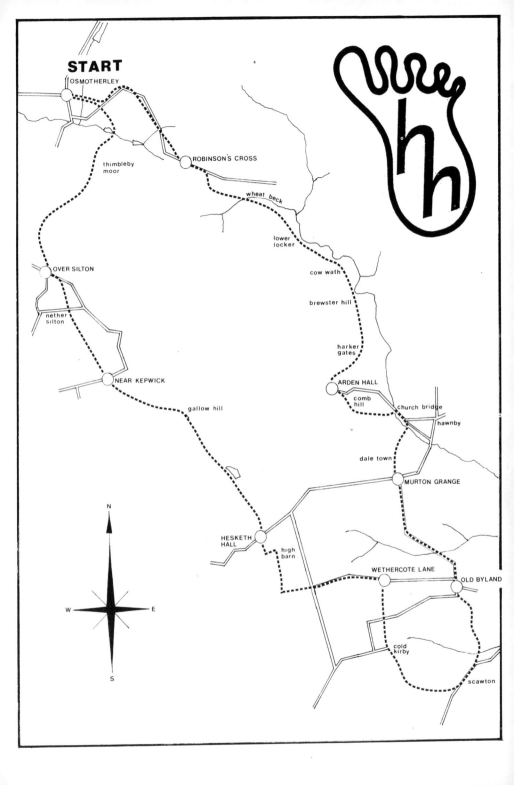

MOORLAND PERSPECTIVE

If he knows anything about the moors he will realise, on reflection, that among many ecological disasters may be listed Bronze Age man himself, for leaving all those burial mounds and sunken trackways behind; the Romans for putting that ugly wide track of rough stones all the way from Cawthorne to the coast; the 18th and 19th Century alum, jet and iron miners whose vast scars still litter the moors; the early warning station and TV mast on Bilsdale West Moor which mean that from any of the moors now some man-made montrosity is in view; the afforestation or agricultural improvement of thousands of acres of heather moor; the bulldozing of fire-break and jeep tracks to shooting butts on many moors which have often destroyed much of archaeological interest and have certainly done more damage than any number of walkers could do.

Bill Cowley in response to a critic of the Lyke Wake Walk

Ralph Cross ▶

MOORLAND MEMORIALS

The Coling Stone
Easington High Moor
Grid Ref NZ 738 104

The William Shaw Stone
Lealholm Rigg
Grid Ref NZ 769 085

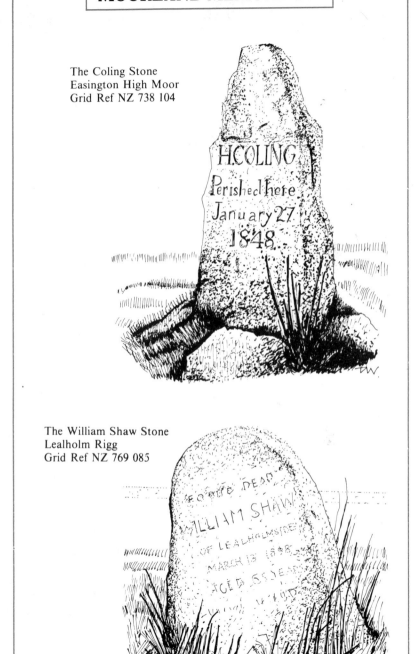

◀ Danby Dale in Summer

HIGH HUNSLEY CIRCUIT   Wolds   24 miles × 1000 feet

Walkington Church 998 368 Circular No time limit
O S Sheet 106 – 1: 50 000
Dennis Parker, 52 Westwood Road, Beverley, Humberside
HU17 8EJ (SAE)
Route Guide

No	Grid Ref	Location	Distance miles	2½ mph pace
1	998 368	Walkington	0	0
2	970 298	Skidby	3	1-10
3	970 298	Wauldby Manor Farm	6	2-35
4	948 298	Brantingham	9	3-35
5	920 317	South Cave	11	4-15
6	935 347	High Hunsley Road	14	5-35
7	940 398	Newbold Lodge	19	7-35
8	987 395	Bishop Burton	22	8-50
9	998 368	Walkington	24	9-50

Dennis Parker, Chairman of the Beverley Group of the Ramblers' Association, inauguarated the High Hunsley Circuit in 1984. The route is well waymarked, easy to follow and is based on definitive rights-of-way. Parts of the route coincide with the Beverley 20 and the Wolds Way. The badge illustrates the BBC's V H F transmitter mast which dominates the skyline throughout much of the walk. A fine day out in some pleasant walking country; a good route for the beginner.

There is about the Wold country a quietness and benignity not elsewhere (I think) to be found in the Shire. It is not the inviolate quietness of the Northern hills; it is not the peace of the remoter dales, but rather a pastoral peace. The scattered villages that lie off the main roads seem to have escaped the tumult and notice of the modern world; they are in the world but not of it; little communities of people living natural, sheltered lives and taking small heed of the march of the affairs beyond.

A. J. Brown
Striding Through Yorkshire, 1938.

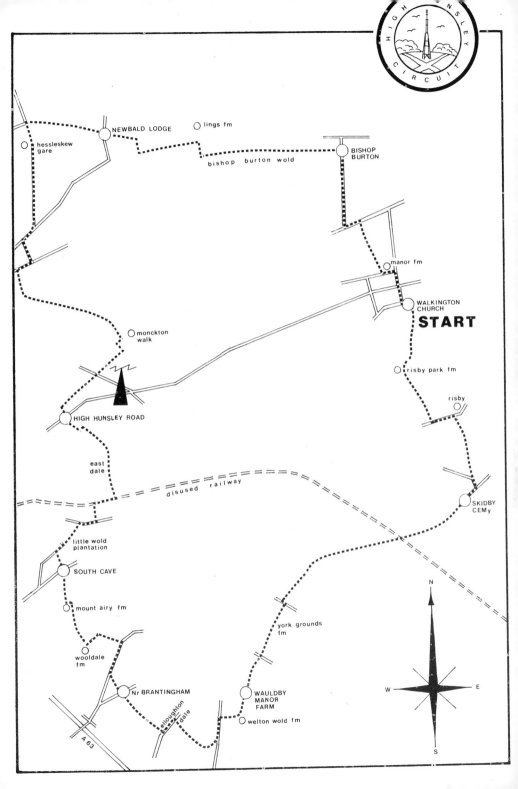

HUMBER BRIDGE LINK   Wolds   30 miles × 500 feet

Hessle Haven 034 256 Circular No time limit
O S Sheets 106, 107, 112 – 1: 50 000
Alf Bushby, 77 Beverley Road, Hessle, Humberside HU13 9AJ (SAE)
Route Guide

No	Grid Ref	Location	Distance miles	2½ mph pace
1	034 258	Hessle Haven	0	0
2	963 246	West Clough	5	2-00
3	960 274	Welton	8	3-15
4	970 298	Wauldby Manor Farm	13	4-25
5	970 291	Welton Wold Farm	15	6-00
6	982 251	Long Plantation	18	7-15
7	025 230	Barton Waterside	22	8-50
8	988 209	South Ferriby	25½	10-15
9	029 195	Kingsforth	30	12-00
10	032 225	Barton-upon-Humber	32½	13-00
11	034 258	Hessle	34	13-35

Just to show that long distance walking appeals to all ages, Alf Bushby devised this figure-of-eight challenge to celebrate his seventieth year in 1984! The route has been designed to link the Wolds Way on the north side of the Humber to the Viking Way in the South. There is no limit and the walk may be completed in one day or in two or more visits. Proceeds from the sale of badges go to help the East Yorkshire Senior Citizens Walkers.

I have seen the Vale of Honiston in Devonshire, that of Taunton and of Glastonbury, in Somersetshire; I have seen the vales of Gloucester and Worcester, and the banks of the Severn and Avon; I have seen the vale of Berkshire, that of Aylesbury, in Buckinghamshire. I have seen the beautiful vales of Wiltshire; and the banks of the Medway, from Tunbridge to Maidstone, called the Garden of Eden. I was born at the end of Arthur Young's 'first ten miles in England'. I have ridden my horse across the Thames at its two sources; and I have seen every inch of its banks from its sources to Gravesend, whence I have sailed out of it into the Channel; and having seen and had the ability to judge of the goodness of the land in all these places I declare that I have never seen any to compare with the land on the banks of the Humber.

William Cobbett
Rural Rides

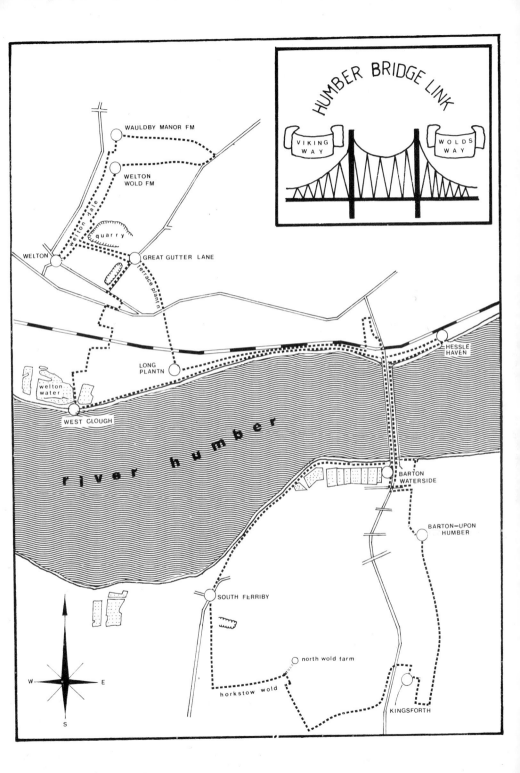

LYKE WAKE WALK   Moors   40 miles × 5 000 feet

Old Quarries Car Park 470 994 Time Limit 24 hours
Raven Hall Hotel 980 018
North York Moors Outdoor Leisure Maps – West and East 1: 25 000
Lyke Wake Club, Goulton Grange, Swainby, Northallerton, North Yorkshire DL6 3HP. (SAE)
Lyke Wake Walk and Lyke Wake Way, Bill Cowley, Dalesman Books 1983
Route Guide

No	Grid Ref	Location	Distance miles	2½ mph pace
1	470 994	Old Quarries Car Park	0	0
2	523 030	Carlton Bank	5	2-00
3	573 033	Hasty Bank	9	3-30
4	616 015	Blowarth Crossing	13	5-15
5	679 020	Rosedale Head	19	7-40
6	744 995	Hamer	23	9-15
7	804 984	Wheeldale	28	11-15
8	857 983	Eller Beck	31	12-25
9	889 987	Lilla Howe	33	13-15
10	945 003	Jugger Howe	37	14-50
11	980 018	Ravenscar	40	16-00

573

"Your feet are killing me" seems to be the message coming from the over-burdened Lyke Wake Walk. Since Bill Cowley first threw down the gauntlet in the Dalesman of August 1955 some 140 000 crossings have been recorded and some sections have become heavily eroded. For those who have not been initiated the walk is a 40 mile traverse of the North York Moors from the most westerly point near Osmotherley to the most easterly point of Ravenscar. Those who complete the route within 24 hours qualify for membership of the Lyke Wake Club. The popularity of the walk should not disguise its difficulties and thorough planning and preparation are the hallmarks of success. Despite some of the problems the walk may have created one cannot deny the benefits or the spirit of adventure that it has inspired in thousands of young people, many of them inexperienced walkers. There is no question of the walk being closed but parties should be limited to ten and go in single file. Large parties should find the recently devised Shepherd's Round and Hambleton Hobble attractive alternatives which have the added convenience of being circular.

LYKE WAKE RACE This is an annual event which takes place each July – see page 59.

LYKE WAKE WAY A longer route based on the walk but allowing completion over a number of days. It does not qualify for the Club badge – see page 79.

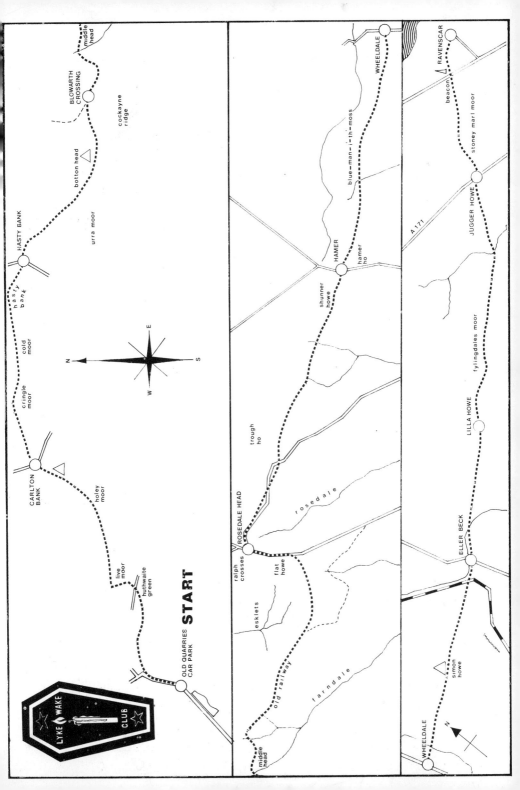

| NORTH WOLDS WALK | Wolds | 20 miles × 1 400 feet |

Lay By A 166, Waytham Farm 836 567 Circular No time limit
O S Sheets 106, 100 – 1: 50 000
The Recorder, North Wolds Walk, Library and Information Service
Reckitt and Colman Pharmaceutical Division, Hull, North Humberside
HU8 7DS (SAE)
Route Guide

No	Grid Ref	Location	Distance miles	2½ mph pace
1	834 569	A 166 Layby	0	0
2	842 610	Thixendale	3	1-15
3	812 608	White Scar Plantation	6	2-25
4	808 586	Kirby Underdale	8	3-15
5	809 567	Garrowby Hill Top	9	3-35
6	797 551	Bishop Wilton	11	4-25
7	812 539	Great Givendale	12	5-00
8	850 544	Millington	14	5-35
9	850 545	Huggate Road	17	6-15
10	834 569	A 166 Layby	20	8-00

Reckitt's Rambling Club promoted this 20 mile challenge in 1982, one of the first in the Yorkshire Wolds. There are no restrictions on how the walk should be completed and it may be done in a day or in two or more sections. The route includes all that is typical in the Wolds – picturesque villages, grassy wolds, valleys and panoramic views. All in all easy going in some pleasant walking country – a good one for the novice long-distance walker.

Kirby Underdale

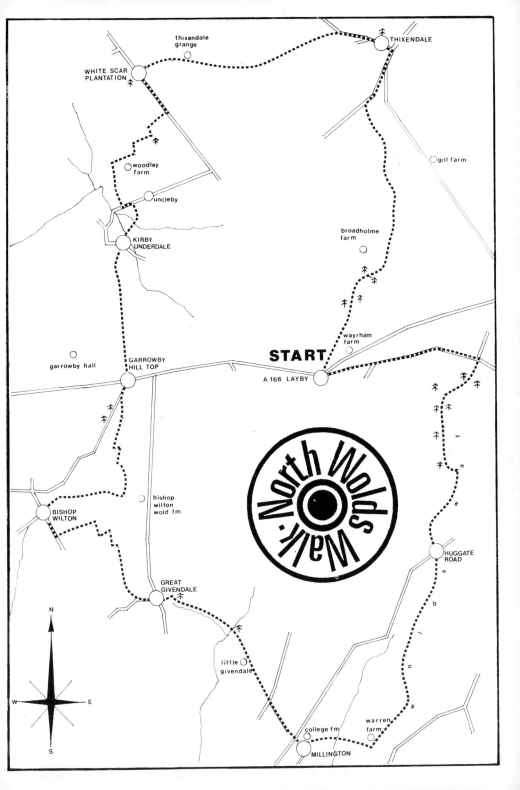

ROSEDALE CIRCUIT   Moors   37 miles × 4 000 feet

Rosedale Abbey 725 959 Circular No time limit
North York Moors Outdoor Leisure Map – West and East 1: 25 000
Rosedale Circuit Secretary, Blackburn Welfare Society, Rambling Club,
British Aerospace, Brough, North Humberside HU15 1EQ. (SAE)
Route Guide

No	Grid Ref	Location	Distance miles	2½ mph pace
1	725 959	Rosedale	0	0
2	692 961	Pike Howe	2	1-00
3	669 975	Church Houses-Farndale	4	1-50
4	640 975	Rudland Rigg	7	2-50
5	624 981	Cow Sike-Bransdale	8	3-30
6	610 001	Incline Top	12	5-00
7	621 068	Baysdale Abbey	15	6-15
8	652 974	Westerdale	19	7-50
9	696 041	Botton Hall-Danby Dale	23	9-15
10	721 035	Wood End Farm-Gt Fryup Dale	25½	10-15
11	734 032	High Dale Farm-Glaisdale	27½	11-00
12	755 011	Wintergill	29½	11-50
13	752 970	High Row Mires	33½	13-30
14	725 959	Rosedale	37	14-50

The route was originated by the Blackburn Welfare Society Rambling Club in 1973. There are no restrictions on how the circuit should be completed though it is recommended that it is walked over two days with an overnight stay in the Westerdale area. An exhilarating and demanding route weaves its way round the heart of the North York Moors to link together Rosedale, Farndale, Bransdale, Westerdale, Danby Dale, Great Fryup Dale and Glaisdale. A notable feature of the walk is that monies received benefit the Campbill Village Trust for the mentally handicapped at Botton Village in Danby Dale. Mention of Danby is a reminder of one of Yorkshire's legendary moorland figures, Canon Christopher John Atkinson, who wrote the scholarly chronicle "Forty Years in a Moorland Parish". As well as being a moorland priest he became a respected historian, naturalist and archaeologist, managed to marry three times, father fourteen children and still found time to walk over 70 000 miles. They do not make vicars like that anymore!

IMPORTANT NOTE In December 1986 enquiries to the walk secretary's address brought no response. Badges etc for this walk may, therefore, be no longer issued. Certificates are still available from Botton Village cafe.

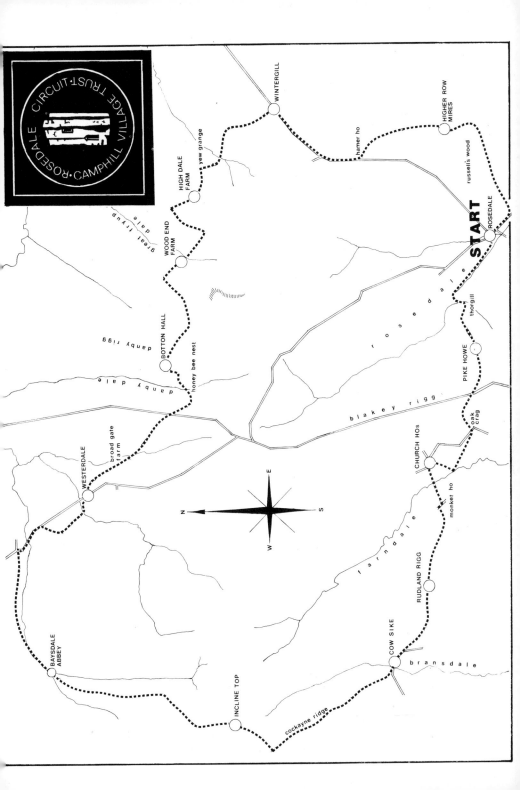

SAMARITAN WAY   Moors   38 miles × 4 500 feet

Guisborough 615 160 Circular 24 hour time limit – optional
North Yorks Moors Outdoor Leisure Map – West and East 1: 25 000
R. T. Pinkney, 11 Pine Road, Ormesby, Middlesbrough, Cleveland (SAE)
Route Guide

No	Grid Ref	Location	Distance miles	2½ mph pace
1	615 160	Guisborough	0	0
2	637 124	Hob on the Hill	3	1-15
3	663 105	Commondale	5	2-00
4	708 086	Danby	9	3-35
5	721 035	Woodend Farm	13	5-15
6	679 020	Rosedale Head	17	6-50
7	656 017	Esklets	22	8-50
8	653 060	Hawthorn House	26	10-25
9	621 068	Baysdale Abbey	29	11-35
10	607 094	Kildale	31	12-25
11	591 110	Gribdale Gate	34	13-35
12	611 138	Highcliffe Nab	36	14-25
13	615 160	Guisborough	38	15-15

The Samaritan Way was officially opened by Lord Guisborough in 1978. The
name of the route is derived from the fact that proceeds from the sale of badges
and certificates are donated to the Teesside Samaritans who maintain a round-the-
clock service for anyone in despair. The walk caters for all tastes with the option of
completing the circuit as a non-stop challenge within 24 hours or in separate
sections. Two different coloured badges are available.

The route has much to commend it. The ever-changing scene from moortop to
secluded dale will delight the eye and draw the feet ever onward. It is one of the
great virtues of long distance walking that it can promote and enrich enjoyment of
the character of the landscape in such a variety of ways. The continuity of walking
allows so many different things to be brought together and contrasted within the
compass of a single day. This circuit exploits such advantage to the full from the
rolling moors, fine ridges and sweeping views to the delectable dales which
characterise this part of the North York Moors. Finally, a word of extreme
caution. Meticulous route planning and careful pacing are necessary to take
advantage of the refreshment facilities offered by the Lion Inn on Blakey Rigg!

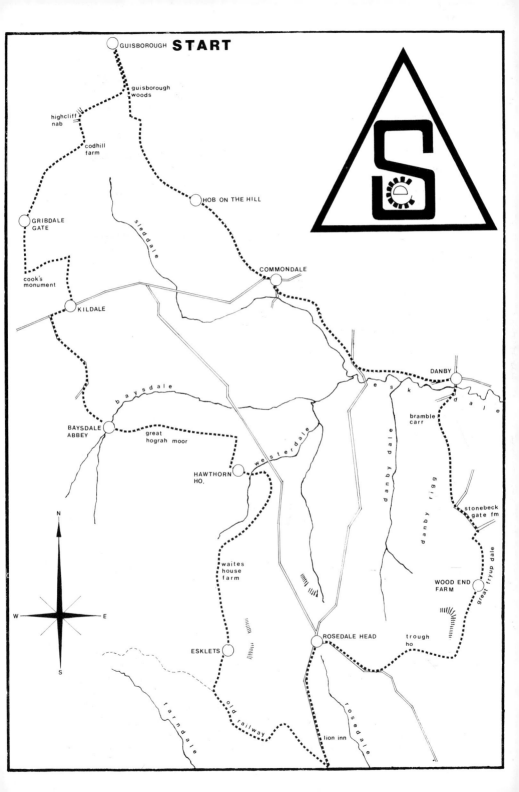

MOORLAND WALKERS

CANON

CHRISTOPHER JOHN ATKINSON

1814 – 1900

Danbydale radiates from the meanderings of the Esk Valley on the North York Moors, and reaches up the fertile valley to the sombre moors at its head. It was in this secluded hamlet during the year 1847 that Canon Atkinson set down his roots and where he acquired an intense love of walking. One can only wonder how an exiled Essex parson could seek asylum in a remote dale where his parishioners still believed in witchcraft, the majority possessing only the basic rudiments of education. During his incumbency there he married three times and had fourteen children, wrote numerous books and prodigiously submitted essays to diverse periodicals, spent considerable hours probing the secrets of bronze age burial mounds and yet still manged to walk over 70 000 miles. In his masterpiece "Forty Years in a Moorland Parish" (1891) he records the following: "Last Sunday I did my duties and walked my ten miles and came in fresh. After my second duty I walked straight away over the moor, out of Fryup, down into Danby, across the dale to see my churchwarden, stricken with paralysis, and home, after the visit, across country, taking walls, hedges and the beck as they came, which is pretty fair for seventy-nine and a half."

Even now to perambulate the hushed lanes of Danbydale or stride the wiry heatherlands above, one can almost sense the presence of the shortsighted vicar probing inquisitively amongst the ling and bracken where he found such immense peace and happiness.

◄ Danby Dale in Winter

MOORLAND WALKERS

A. J. BROWN

1894 – 1969

"Every man who tramps will find his own crock of gold" so writes that indefatigable moorland-tramper and author, Alfred John Brown. Born in Bradford in 1894 he acquired from an early age a passion for walking by taking regular jaunts with his father that were to sustain him throughout his lifetime. When he was cruelly struck down by diphtheria in his youth it only renewed his determination to seek out the high and lonely places; he knew walking was his real salvation. He recovered to be overtaken by a restless wanderlust that urged him to perambulate the majority of English shires, though he was never happier than wallowing across the whams and hags of some rough windswept Yorkshire moor, or tracing the sinuous flow of some river to its source.

In his classic tomes – Striding through Yorkshire, 1938, Broad Acres, 1949, and Fair North Riding, 1952 – the language of moor, dale and fell are evocatively painted in A.J.'s breezy style. Although there is now a plethora of books of walking, many devotees of the walking fraternity still scour the shelves of secondhand bookshops to discover a treasured volume of A.J. Brown's. But even Yorkshire's 'Prince of Walkers' offers this warning:– "Rest assured, you will not experience the ecstasies in an easychair by the fireside! Tramping is an active delight which only those who practise can rightly apprehend. But up there on the 'tops' – away from all books (and slippers), away from all sects (and cities) – it is there for the finding. And every man who tramps will find his own secret crock of gold."

Staithes ▶

SCARBOROUGH ROCK   Moors   26 miles × 2 000 feet

Peasholm Car Park 035 897 Circular 12 hour limit

O.S. Sheet 101 – 1: 50 000 Moors Outdoor Leisure Map – East 1: 25 000

Mr M. Ellis, 77 Worthing Street, Clough Road, Hull HU5 1PP (SAE)

Route Guide

No	Grid Ref	Location	Distance miles	2½ mph pace
1	035 897	Peasholm Car Park	0	0
2	040 870	Oliver's Mount	3	1-15
3	009 876	Seamer Beacon	6	2-25
4	984 876	Forge Valley Picnic Site	8	3-25
5	967 906	Hackness	13	5-15
6	965 944	Reasty Bank	17	6-50
7	986 939	Kirklees Farm	18	7-15
8	027 935	Burniston Cliff Top	22	8-50
9	035 897	Peasholm Car Park	26	10-25

The Scarborough Rock added yet more colour and diversity to the challenge walk scene when it was launched by the East Yorkshire Group of the Long Distance Walkers Association in 1982. Even those familiar with Scarborough through annual seaside pilgrimages will return from this walk with deeper memories and a fresher perspective of this friendly coastal resort and its little-frequented hinterland. The route starts by taking in the twin bays of Scarborough, passing many of its grand old hotels, a reminder of more glorious days, to the ancient castle and the parish church. A steep descent and a taste of bygone Scarborough leads to the busy fishing harbour before crossing the sandy beach to make the ascent of Oliver's Mount with its sweeping view back across the bay. The Mere, Rowbrow and Raincliffe Woods follow on to the wooded glades of Forge Valley, and then Hackness. The combination of the village, its fine hall, park and lake, against a setting of woods and hills, make it a memorable spot. Beyond Hackness, Low Dales Beck leads into a world of miniature dales, wooded hillocks, soft contours and solitary farmsteads. The walk ascends the curiously named Whisperdales to Reasty Bank. Country lanes then cross to Burniston where the clifftop path weaves and dips its way towards the headland silhouette of Scarborough Castle and back to the North Bay.

CHALLENGE EVENT An organised challenge event takes place each January – see page 55.

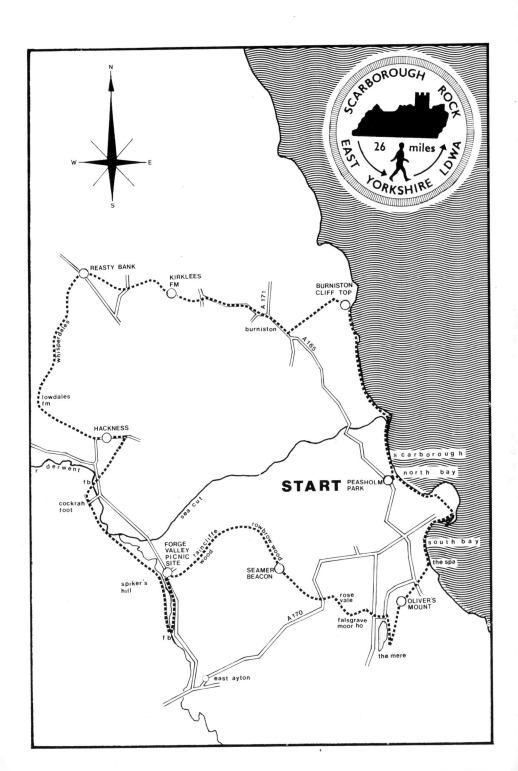

SCARBOROUGH SAMARITANS Moors 25 miles × 1 000 feet

Scalby 009 904 Circular 12 hours limit

North York Moors Outdoor Leisure Map – East 1: 25 000

Keith, The Samaritans, 35a St. Nicholas Cliff, Scarborough, North Yorkshire (SAE)

Route Guide

No	Grid Ref	Location	Distance miles	2½ mph pace
1	009 904	Scalby	0	0
2	969 893	Wrench Green	3½	1-25
3	943 910	Langdale Bridge	6	2-25
4	936 951	Harewood Dale	9	3-25
5	949 965	Chapel Farm	11	4-25
6	949 000	A171	14	5-35
7	982 018	Ravenscar	16	6-25
8	007 969	Hayburn Wyke	20	8-00
9	017 928	Burniston	23	9-15
10	009 904	Scalby	25	10-00

First promoted in 1984, this is another route devised to relieve pressure from the Lyke Wake Walk. The walk is specially designed to attract walkers who wish to do a sponsored walk by providing a ready made charity to support as well as a route. Monies from the walk provide vital support to the Scarborough Samaritans Centre which provides a 24 hour service for anyone in despair, handles 3 500 calls a year and is manned by some 70 volunteers. As well as supporting a worthy cause the circuit offers an excellent opportunity to sample all that is best in Yorkshire's scenery, combining dale, wood, moor and coast into an attractive walk.

CHALLENGE EVENT An organised event takes place each September – see page 63.

> I nearly always come to this point on the cliffs to watch the sea. It does me a world of good – a breath of fresh air, you know, and all the wideness of the horizon instead of a brick wall facing my kitchen. And the music! I am not sure I should be able to keep on all summer through if I did not get an hour off sometimes – an hour by the sea, alone with the bigness of it, and my thoughts.
>
> **By a woman who ran a Scarborough boarding house in the 1930's**

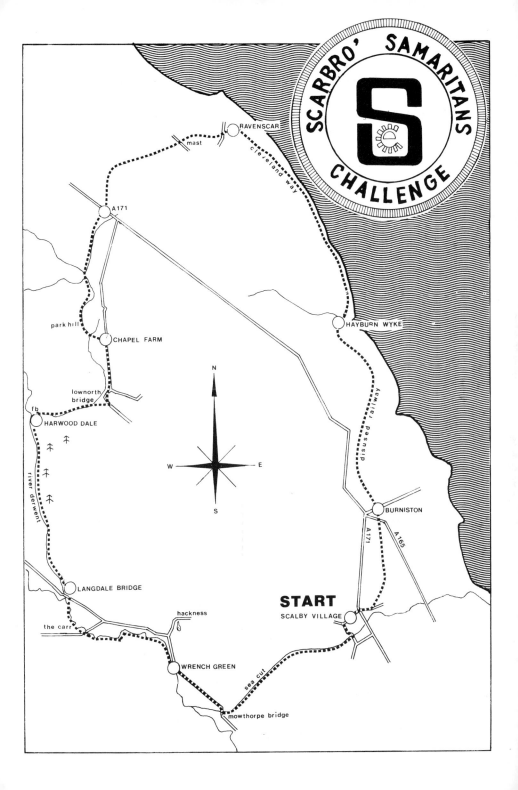

SEAHORSE SAUNTER	Moors	43 miles × 5 000 feet

White Horse 515 814 Whitby 901 113 24 hours limit

North York Moors Outdoor Leisure Maps – West and East 1: 25 000

S. Watkins, 36 Barons Crescent, St. Giles Park, Copmanthorpe, York YO2 3TZ. (SAE)

Route Guide

No	Grid Ref	Location	Distance miles	2½ mph pace
1	515 814	White Horse	0	0
2	530 845	Cold Kirby	3	1-10
3	564 888	Newgate Bank	9	3-35
4	622 945	Stork House	15	6-00
5	669 975	Church Houses	22	8-50
6	714 017	Fryup Head	26	10-25
7	804 051	Egton Bridge	34	13-35
8	901 113	Whitby	43	17-10

Launched in 1985 the Seahorse Saunter is the latest and longest anytime challenge to grace the North York Moors. No walking guide would be complete without a visit to Whitby, the picturesque seaside resort famous for its clifftop abbey and associations with St. Hilda and Caedmon, the first English Christian poet. The pilgrimage begins far away at the foot of the steps leading to the White Horse of Kilburn; it finishes at the top of the infamous 199 steps overlooking Whitby harbour. In between a kaleidoscope of moor and dale stretches 43 miles across the heart of the North York Moors. All in all an inspiring traverse of a fine landscape, demanding sound experience, stamina and training.

Whitby

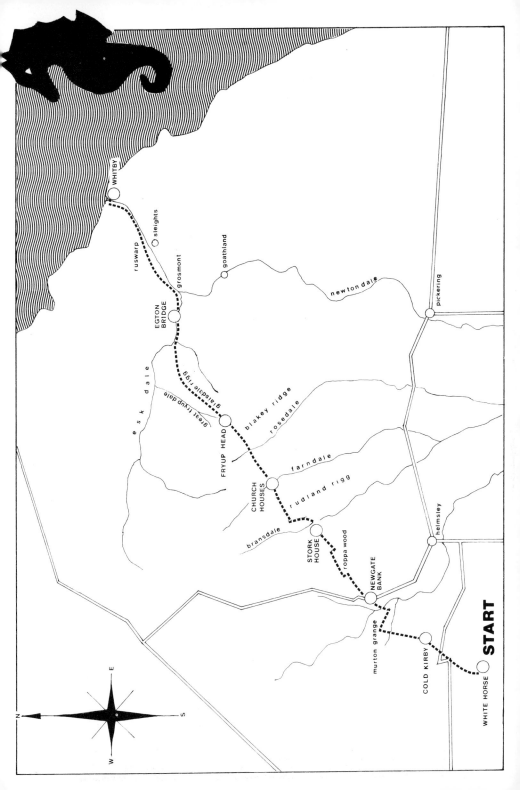

SHEPHERD'S ROUND Moors 36 miles × 5 000 feet

Old Quarries Car Park 470 994 Circular 24 hours limit (optional)
North York Moors Outdoor Leisure Map – West 1: 25 000
Lyke Wake Club, Goulton Grange, Swainby, Northallerton DL6 3HP (SAE)
Route Guide

No	Grid Ref	Location	Distance miles	2½ mph pace
1	470 994	Old Quarries Car Park	0	0
2	523 030	Carlton Bank	5	2-00
3	513 033	Hasty Bank	9	3-35
4	616 015	Blowarth Crossing	13	5-15
5	622 984	Cockayne	16	6-25
6	569 946	Fangdale Beck	21	8-25
7	543 898	Hawnby	26	10-25
8	491 931	Whitestones	31	12-25
9	470 994	Old Quarries Car Park	36	14-25

This circuit was first suggested by Alan Neasham of Osmotherley as an alternative to the Lyke Wake Walk and promoted by Bill Cowley in his 1983 edition of the Lyke Wake Walk book. There is no time limit and the route may be tackled as a 24 hour challenge or as a two day outing with overnight accommodation at Fangdale Beck or Hawnby. A gold badge is available for a sub 24 hour circuit and a green for over 24 hours. The walk is over ancient footpaths and bridleways and offers firm going suitable for large parties. The Lyke Wake Club advise that the Bransdale to Bilsdale and Fangdale Beck to Honey Hill sections are not well marked and could be difficult. The Round provides another strenuous challenge that should only be undertaken by well equipped, trained and experienced walkers.

> I dreamt last night of England and the rain,
> grey clouds across the Yorkshire hills, and mist
> haunting the moors, curled low in every grain;
> close huddled sheep keeping bedraggled tryst
> behind a broken wall; a smell of wet heather;
> music of rushing streams; beat of the wind;
> one solitary shepherd . . . "Mucky weather!"
> . . . "Aye, dampish . . . an' ah've
> three young lambs ti find".
>
> **Bill Cowley (while in India)**

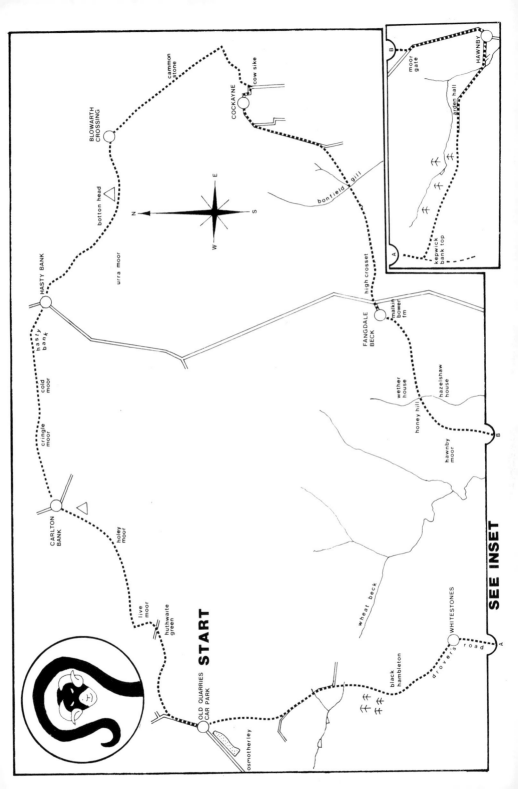

SEE INSET

START

Inset labels:
HAWNBY
moor gate
B
arden hall
kepwick bank top
A

Main map labels:
cammon stone
BLOWARTH CROSSING
cow sike
COCKAYNE
botton head
urra moor
bonfield gill
HASTY BANK
hasty bank
high crosset
FANGDALE BECK
malkin bower fm
cold moor
cringle moor
wether house
honey hill
hazelshaw house
hawnby moor
CARLTON BANK
holey moor
B
live moor
huthwaite green
wheat beck
OLD QUARRIES CAR PARK
osmotherley
black hambleton
drovers road
WHITESTONES
A

WHITE ROSE WALK   Moors   31 miles × 4 000 feet

Newton-Under-Roseberry 571 128 White Horse, Kilburn 514 813
No time limit North York Moors Outdoor Leisure Map – West Sheet 1: 25 000
Mr G.E. Garbutt, 17 Kingsclere, Huntington, York YO3 9SF. (SAE)
The White Rose Walk, Geoffrey White, Dalesman 1980
Route Guide – for short route

No	Grid Ref	Location	Distance miles	2½ mph pace
1	571 128	Newton under Roseberry	0	0
2	607 094	Kildale	5	2-00
3	595 016	Botton Head	12	4-50
4	559 997	Chop Gate	15	6-00
5	534 971	Head House	17	6-50
6	510 945	Wheat Beck	20	8-00
7	491 931	White Stones	22	8-50
8	508 875	Sneck Yate	26	10-25
9	514 813	White Horse	31	12-30

This walk was devised by the Yorkshire Wayfarers Rambling Club and first completed in 1968. It connects the two prominent landmarks of Roseberry Topping and the White Horse of Kilburn in a tough traverse of the Cleveland and Hambleton Hills. The route is appropriately divided into the roseberry, the foliage and the stem. The foliage, the middle section between Botton Head and Whitestones, provides the option of a long, medium and short route. The short 31 mile route has proved the most popular both because of the distance and the mid-day break offered by the Buck Inn at Chop Gate. As well as Roseberry Topping, the little green alp of the North York Moors, the walk visits the obelisk erected to Captain Cook, Yorkshire's celebrated seaman, born over 250 years ago in sight of these rugged hills.

In Memory of Captain Cook
The celebrated circumnavigator
A man in nautical knowledge inferior to none in Zeal,
Prudence and Energy superior to Most Regardless of Danger
he opened an Intercourse with the Friendly Isles
and other parts of the Southern hemisphere.
Born at Marton in 1728.
Massacred at Owhyee 1779.

Inscription on Monument Hill

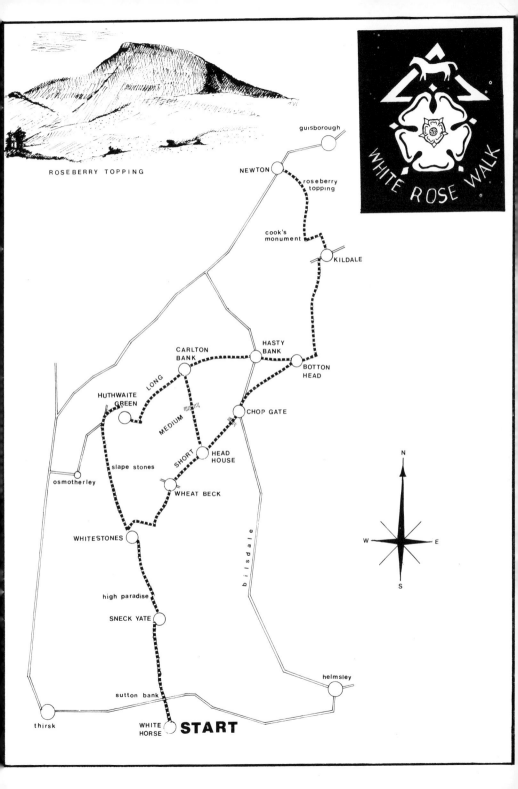

ROSEBERRY TOPPING

WHITE ROSE WALK

guisborough

NEWTON

roseberry topping

cook's monument

KILDALE

CARLTON BANK

HASTY BANK

BOTTON HEAD

LONG

HUTHWAITE GREEN

MEDIUM

CHOP GATE

SHORT

HEAD HOUSE

slape stones

osmotherley

WHEAT BECK

WHITESTONES

bilsdale

high paradise

SNECK YATE

helmsley

sutton bank

thirsk

WHITE HORSE

START

N

W   E

S

OTHER CHALLENGES

MONKS' TROD – An alternative to the Lyke Wake Walk for large parties and sponsored walks put forward by Bill Cowley in the 1983 edition of the Lyke Wake Walk. Approximately 20 miles between Byland Abbey and Rievaulx. If demand is sufficient a badge and certificate will be issued.

RAIL TRAIL – A 20-26 mile walk in Eskdale between Battersby and Glaisdale making use of British Rail to get to the start. Another alternative to the Lyke Wake Walk suggested by Bill Cowley in his 1983 edition. Badge and certificate subject to demand.

THREE FEATHERS WALK – This requires the completion of three different routes each within a different National Park. All the walks must be completed within the twelve month period between January 1 and December 31.

The first feather is a 30 mile circuit based on Kettlewell, the second a 30 mile circuit of the North York Moors from the White Horse at Kilburn. The third feather is a 26 mile walk in the Peak District from Yorkshire Bridge. Badge and certificate. Send a large stamped addressed envelope to: the 'Bards Recorder', Keith Brown, Dale House, 35 Bawtry Road, Listerdale, Rotherham S66 0AR.

HUTTON HIKE
RUDSTON ROAM
HEADLAND WALK
These walks are all sections of the East Riding Heritage Way recreational path. They can also be undertaken as separate challenge walks to be completed within a 12 hour time limit to qualify for a badge. See page 73 for details and addresses.

J.M. MOORS CHALLENGE –
Another in the long line of John Merrill's commercial promotions. A 24 mile circuit from Goathland over to Robin Hood's Bay and back. Badge and certificate available. **John Merrill's, North Yorkshire Moors Challenge Walk, John Merrill, JNM Publications, 1986.**

RING OF IRON – A proposed 42 miles circuit of Cleveland's Iron Age heritage, badge and certificate. Details from M. Power, 38 Exter Road, Eston, Cleveland TS6 9PF (SAE).

LANGBRAUGH LOOP – A proposed 38 miles circuit. Details from Mr P. G. Thompson, Jordans Guest House, 15 Pearl Street, Saltburn-by-the-sea, Cleveland.

CHALLENGES PAST

The walks below have been discontinued due to potential erosion problems. Badges and certificates are no longer issued.

WEST CLEVELAND CIRCUIT

NYMROD – North York Moors Route of the Dales, superseded by the Rosedale Circuit (page 32)

EVENTS

A Calendar of Walks which are organised annually on specific dates and for which Badges and Certificates are awarded

The Cleveland Classic

CHALLENGE EVENTS
CALENDAR

miles

January	Scarborough Rock Winter Challenge	26
January	Wheeldale Tandem	27
March	Cleveland Survival	26
April	Flamborough Fling	25
May	Saltersgate Circuit	26
May	Windmill Way	26
June	Levisham Limp	30
July	Crosses Walk	54
July	Lyke Wake Race	40
August	West Cleveland Round	28
August	Smuggler's Trod	26
September	Cleveland Classic	56
September	Ings Marathon	26
September	Scarborough Samaritans Challenge	26
September	Falcon Flyer	26
October	Pathfinder 25	25
October	Hesierton Hump	21
November	Kilburn Kanter	25

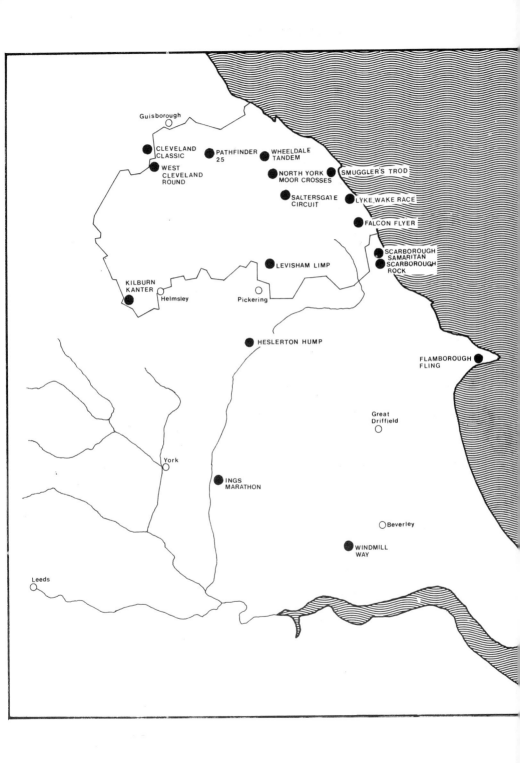

EVENTS

- Date and start time are fixed
- Entry by application form and fee
- Maximum number of participants
- Route is defined by a series of checkpoints where tallies must be punched. Drinks are available at some checkpoints
- Rules to specify both equipment to carry and conduct
- Certificate awarded for completion, badge often available
- Individual and team trophies are often awarded
- Time limit allowing all but the slowest to finish
- Results sheet is usually published
- Essentially a sporting challenge although a competitive element usually exists
- Walkers are not sponsored. The proceeds from many walks go to help local charities, rescue services or scout groups
- While all information was up-to-date at the time of publication the addresses of walk secretaries can change. For the latest information membership of the Long Distance Walkers Association is recommended. They provide a comprehensive information service by way of a magazine which includes a regular calendar of events and reports of past events. See page 93
- A standard format has been used in displaying information in this section as shown below.

SCARBOROUGH ROCK　　26 miles × 10 hours　　**JANUARY**
name of event　　　　　　*distance, maximum time allowed*　　　　*month*

OS Sheet 101 – 1 : 50000
map　　　　　*scale*

Badge, Certificate, Meal, Trophies
awards etc

Organised by East Yorkshire Long Distance Walkers Association
organiser

M. Ellis, 77 Worthing Street, Clough Street, Hull, Humberside HU5 1PP (SAE)
Walk Secretary from whom to obtain entry form and details ALWAYS ENCLOSE A LARGE SAE. Apply up to six months in advance to ensure a place.

No.	Grid Ref	Checkpoints	
S	024 898	St Mark's Scout Hut	*Marshalled checkpoints*
1	038 897	Corner Cafe	*through which each walker*
2	048 891	Castle	*must pass using the route*
3	044 880	Spa	*description provided by the*
4	039 870	Oliver's Mount	*organisers or by using rights*
5	035 857	Scarborough Mere	*of way.*
6	019 869	Jacob's Mount	*Refreshments are available*
7	007 883	Rowbrow-Raincliffe Woods	*at some checkpoints.*
8	984 876	Forge Valley Picnic Site	*The checkpoints shown were*
9	974 906	Hackness Hall	*current at publication but*
10	968 906	Hackness Lowdales Beck	*may be varied in future*
11	964 915	Broxa	*events.*
12	965 994	Reasty Bank	
13	016 931	Burniston (Lane/Railway)	
F	024 898	St Mark's Scout Hut	

SCARBOROUGH ROCK 26 miles × 10 hours **JANUARY**

OS Sheet 101 – 1: 50000
Badge, Certificate, Meal, Trophies
Organised by East Yorkshire Long Distance Walkers Association
M. Ellis, 77 Worthing Street, Clough Street, Hull, Humberside HU5 1PP
(SAE)

No.	Grid Ref	Checkpoints
S	024 898	St Mark's Scout Hut
1	038 897	Corner Cafe
2	048 891	Castle
3	044 880	Spa
4	039 870	Oliver's Mount
5	035 857	Scarborough Mere
6	019 869	Jacob's Mount
7	007 883	Rowbrow-Raincliffe Woods
8	984 876	Forge Valley Picnic Site
9	974 906	Hackness Hall
10	968 906	Hackness Lowdales Beck
11	964 915	Broxa
12	965 994	Reasty Bank
13	016 931	Burniston (Lane/Railway)
F	024 898	St Mark's Scout Hut

WHEELDALE TANDEM 27 miles × 11 hours **JANUARY**

North York Moors Outdoor Leisure Maps – 1:25 000
Badge, Certificate, Meal, Prizes
For teams of two, each taking seperate routes as far as Wheeldale
Organised by Cleveland Long Distance Walkers Association
Mr B. Pearson, 29 Marway Road, Botton, Saltburn-by-the-Sea, Cleveland

No.	Grid Ref	East Checkpoints	No.	Grid Ref	West Checkpoints
S	830 053	Grosmont	S	830 053	Grosmont
1	837 069	Old Park Lane	1	793 046	Delves
2	868 081	Sleights Station	2	763 076	Lealholm
3	880 050	Littlebeck	3	721 059	Forresters Lodge
4	891 023	May Beck Car Park	4	715 053	Stonebeck Gate Fm
5	931 994	Juggerhowe Beck	5	729 028	Glaisdale Moor
6	857 982	Ellerbeck Bridge	6	706 010	Boundary Post
7	813 984	Wheeldale Y.H.	7	744 995	Hamer Road
8	827 007	Mallyan Spout Hotel	8	813 984	Wheeldale Y.H.
F	830 053	Grosmont	9	827 007	Mallyan Spout Hotel
			F	830 053	Grosmont

CLEVELAND SURVIVAL   26 miles × 11 hours   **MARCH**

North York Moors Area
Badge, Certificate, Meal, Prizes
Organised by the Cleveland Search and Rescue Team
Walk Secretary, 7 Southfield Close, Hurworth, Darlington,
Co. Durham DL2 2ER (SAE)

A different route is selected each year. Venue plus details of accommodation and transport are sent out approximately four weeks before the event, but the route is not disclosed until the actual day. Open to runners and walkers.

FLAMBOROUGH FLING   25 miles × 9 hours   **APRIL**

O S Sheet 101 – 1: 50 000
Badge, Certificate, Meal
Organised by Bridlington Boys Club
D. Harper, 22 Thoresby Avenue, Bridlington, North Humberside,
YO16 5EL (SAE)

No.	Grid Ref	Checkpoints
S	195 680	Bridlington Car Park
1	170 643	Wilsthorpe
2	136 669	Woldgate
3	131 710	Grindale Village
4	181 723	Buckton Crossing
5	196 738	Bempton Bird Sanctuary
6	239 720	Flamborough North Landing
7	255 706	Flamborough Lighthouse
8	232 693	Flamborough South Landing
F	195 680	Bridlington Car Park

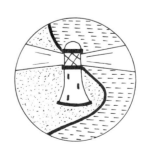

SALTERSGATE CIRCUIT   26 miles × 12 hours   **MAY**

O S Sheet 94 – 1: 50 000
Badge, Certificate
Organised by Scarborough Search and Rescue Team
Mrs M. Ingram, 99 York Road, Driffield, East Yorks YO25 7AY (SAE)

No.   Grid Ref   Checkpoints

S	845 882	Fox and Rabbit Inn
1	829 884	Farwith
2	820 916	Levisham Moor
3	785 921	Cawthorn Moor
4	802 972	Rutmore Beck
5	831 981	Simon Howe
6	841 954	Needle Point
7	852 938	Saltersgate Bank Top
8	867 949	Malo Cross
9	875 904	Bridestones Car Park
F	845 882	Fox and Rabbit Inn

WINDMILL WAY   26 miles × 10 hours   **MAY**

O S Sheet 106 – 1: 50 000
Badge, Certificate
Organised by 1st Skidby Scouts
Mrs A. Gray, 15 The Butts, Little Weighton, Cottingham, North Humberside
HU20 3XD (SAE)

No.   Grid Ref   Checkpoints

S	984 339	Little Weighton
1	963 329	Riplingham
2	937 331	Weedley
3	907 319	Everthorpe
4	924 310	South Cave
5	944 301	Brantingham
6	955 278	Welton
7	976 315	York Grounds
8	021 333	Skidby Windmill
9	015 337	Skidby
10	003 347	Risby
F	984 339	Little Weighton

WINDMILL WAY

LEVISHAM LIMP   30 miles × 12 hours   **JUNE**

O S Sheet 94 – 1: 50 000
Badge, Certificate, Meal
Organised by 42nd St. Marks Venture Scout Unit, Scarborough
John March, 165 Scalby Road, Scarborough, North Yorkshire (SAE)

No.	Grid Ref	Checkpoints
S	833 904	Levisham Village Hall
1	827 952	Forest Drive
2	813 984	Wheeldale Lodge
3	811 021	Randy Mere
4	762 016	Wintergill Plantation
5	725 977	Northdale Rigg
6	726 955	Rosedale
7	789 936	Stape
F	833 904	Levisham Village Hall

LYKE WAKE RACE   40 miles × 12 hours   **JULY**

North York Moors Outdoor Leisure maps – East and West – 1: 25 000
Certificate and Trophies
Organised in conjunction with the Osmotherley Summer Games
Lyke Wake Race Secretary, Witsend, South Kilvington, Thirsk
North Yorkshire YO7 2NF (SAE)

First staged in 1964, the race has taken place each July since. Participants have different handicap times and start from Ravenscar at varying intervals to finish in Osmotherley village where the games are in progress. Entry open only to those who have previously completed the walk.

ROUTE see LYKE WAKE WALK – page 28.

CROSSES WALK   54 miles × 24 hours   JULY

North York Moors Outdoor Leisure Maps – West and East 1: 25 000
Badge, Certificate, Meal, Trophies
Organised by the Scarborough and District Search and Rescue Team
Mrs B. Hood, 21 St Peter's Street, Norton, Malton, North Yorkshire (SAE)

No.	Grid Ref	Checkpoints
S	830 012	Goathland
1	755 012	Wintergill
2	742 030	Glaisdale Road
3	697 019	Botton Cross
4	677 021	Ralph's Cross – East
5	673 019	Ralph's Cross – West
6	722 948	Rosedale Chimney
7	734 882	Low Cross
8	796 943	Mauley Cross
9	852 940	Saltersgate Bank Top
10	866 949	Malo Cross
11	889 987	Lilla Cross
12	922 045	Postgate Cross
13	900 026	John Cross
14	879 015	York Cross
F	830 012	Goathland

Checkpoint halt

WEST CLEVELAND ROUND   28 miles × 11 hours   AUGUST

North York Moors Outdoor Leisure Maps West – 1: 25 000
Badge, Certificate, Trophies
For teams of two, each taking separate red and green after six miles
at Round Hill
Organised by Cleveland Long Distance Walkers Association
Alan Peverell, 54 Tavistock Road, Linthorpe, Middlesbrough,
Cleveland TS6 6ER (SAE)

No.	Grid Ref	Red Route	Grid Ref	Green Route
S	581 063	Ingleby Greenhow	581 063	Ingleby Greenhow
1	616 015	Bloworth Crossing	616 015	Bloworth Crossing
2	594 016	Round Hill	594 016	Round Hill
3	559 993	Chop Gate	573 036	Clay Bank
4	534 973	Nr Head House	560 035	Wainstones
5	519 026	Carlton Bank	535 034	Cringle Moor
6	535 034	Cringle Moor	519 026	Carlton Bank
7	560 035	Wainstones	534 973	Nr Head House
8	573 036	Clay Bank	559 993	Chop Gate
9	616 015	Bloworth Crossing	616 015	Bloworth Crossing
10	604 061	Battersby Moor	604 061	Battersby Moor
F	581 063	Ingleby Greenhow	581 063	Ingleby Greenhow

SMUGGLER'S TROD   26 miles × 10½ hours   AUGUST

North York Moors Outdoor Leisure Map East – 1: 25 000
Badge, Certificate, Meal
Organised by Yorkshire Coast LDWA
Mrs M. Atkinson, Fulmer Cottage, Stoupe Brow, Ravenscar, Nr Scarborough,
North Yorkshire (SAE)

No.	Grid Ref	Checkpoints	No.	Grid Ref	Checkpoint
S	949 054	Flyingdales Village Hall	11	937 019	Ford
1	938 058	Raw Lane	12	969 012	Radio Mast
2	933 046	Thornfield Farm	13	956 024	Fulmar Cottage
3	916 029	Whitby Road	14	943 026	Monks Steps
4	893 024	May Becks	15	927 028	St Ives Pond
5	886 040	Hermitage	16	936 043	Fylinghall
6	860 024	Boundary Stones	17	953 048	The Dock RHB
7	886 992	Louven Howe	F	949 054	Fylingdales Village Hall
8	895 002	Leech Bog Slack			
9	914 000	Hollin Gill			
10	931 007	Flask Inn			

CLEVELAND CLASSIC 56 miles × 24 hours   SEPTEMBER

O S Sheets 93, 94 – 1: 50 000

Badge, Certificate, Meal, Trophies

Organised on behalf of The Camphill Village Trust

Mrs M. Hutchinson, 13 Buckingham Drive, Normanby, Middlesbrough
Cleveland TS6 0QD (SAE)

No.	Grid Ref	Checkpoints
S	564 113	Great Ayton
1	579 126	Roseberry Topping
2	640 159	Slapewith
3	670 216	Saltburn
4	700 213	Skinningrove-North
5	745 199	Skinningrove-South
6	782 189	Staithes
7	755 170	Roxby Woods
8	756 129	Scaling Dam
9	736 093	Danby Beacon
10	710 062	Danby Rigg
11	695 043	Botton Village
12	616 014	Bloworth Crossing
13	610 084	Park Dyke
14	592 110	Gribdale
15	597 126	Roseberry Topping
F	564 113	Great Ayton

INGS MARATHON   26 miles × 12 hours   SEPTEMBER

O S Sheets 105 or 106 – 1: 50 000

Certificate, Meal, Trophies

Organised on behalf of the Parish Churches of Elvington, Sutton Upon
Derwent and East Cottingwith

Mr R.A. Starks, 1 The Green, Elvington, York, YO4 5AF (SAE)

No.	Grid Ref	Checkpoints
S	707 472	Sutton Village Hall
1	691 469	Nr Elvington Wood
2	707 444	Nr Sutton Farm
3	699 403	Ellerton Landing
4	748 446	Nr Melbourne
5	768 475	Allerthorpe Common
6	738 484	Nr Gale House
F	707 472	Suttin Village Hall

SCARBOROUGH SAMARITANS CHALLENGE
25 miles × 12 hours   SEPTEMBER

North York Moors Outdoor Leisure Map, East – 1: 25 000
Badge, Certificate, Trophies
Organised by Scarborough Samaritans – Sponsorship Preferred
Keith, The Samaritans, 35a St. Nicholas Cliff, Scarborough,
North Yorkshire (SAE)

No.	Grid Ref	Checkpoints
S	009 904	Scalby
1	969 893	Nr Wrench Green
2	943 910	Langdale End
3	936 951	Low North Beck
4	949 968	Footbridge
5	949 000	Scarboro. – Whitby Road
6	982 018	Raven Hall
7	007 969	Hayburn Wyke Hotel
8	017 928	Disused Railway
F	009 904	Scalby

FALCON FLYER   26 miles × 12 hours   SEPTEMBER

O S Sheet 94 – 1: 50 000
Badge, Certificate, T-shirt
Organised by Scarborough and District Search and Rescue Team
Mrs M. Ingram, 99 York Rd., Driffield, East Yorks YO25 7AY

No.	Grid Ref	Checkpoints
S	971 981	Falcon Inn
1	947 983	Watersmeet
2	919 010	Biller How Dale
3	899 015	John Bond's Sheephouse
4	891 025	May Beck Car Park
5	880 049	Little Beck
6	892 064	Laund House JCT
7	932 075	Hawkser
8	940 083	Hawkser
9	951 055	Robin Hood's Bay
10	960 025	Stoupe Brow
11	980 016	Ravenscar
12	972 004	Green Lane
F	971 981	Falcon Inn

PATHFINDER 25   25 miles × 10 hours   OCTOBER

O S Sheet 106 – 1: 50 000

Badge, Certificate, Meal

Organised by 25th Middlesbrough Pathfinder Scouts

Mrs R. Chambers, 84 Bournemouth Avenue, Ormesby, Middlesbrough
Cleveland TS3 0NR (SAE)

No.	Grid Ref	Checkpoints
S	661 107	Ravengill Camp
1	663 107	Site Commondale
2	713 116	Robin Hood Butts
3	717 085	Danby Lodge
4	711 055	Crossley House
5	695 046	Road to Botton
6	659 066	Above Westerdale
7	626 075	"Y" of Baysdale
8	613 113	Kildale Moor
F	661 107	Commondale HQ

HESLERTON HUMP   21 miles × 8 hours   OCTOBER

O S Sheet SE 87/97 Rillington & Sherburn – 1: 25 000

Certificate, Prizes, Meal

Organised for St Andrews Church, East Heslerton by P.W. Stead

P.W. Stead, Heathfield, Carr Lane, East Heslerton, Malton, North Yorkshire
YO17 8RP (SAE)

No.	Grid Ref	Checkpoints
S	926 767	East Heslerton Church
1	930 729	Whinmoor Farm
2	895 697	Rayslack Farm
3	911 747	West Heslerton Brow
F	926 767	East Heslerton Church

KILBURN KANTER   25 miles × 10 hours   **NOVEMBER**

O S Sheet 106 – 1: 50 000
Badge, Certificate
Organised by North Yorkshire L.D.W.A.
Derek Haller, 11 Cambridge Terrace, Otley, West Yorkshire, LS21 1JS (SAE)

No.	Grid Ref	Checkpoint
S	514 796	Kilburn Village Hall
1	515 813	White Horse
2	504 833	Gormire Lake
3	488 866	Boltby Village
4	482 896	Seta Pike
5	494 923	Lime Kiln House
6	525 905	Arden Hall
7	542 889	Hawnby
8	568 855	Nr Bow Bridge
9	552 819	A 170
10	530 799	Oldstead
F	514 796	Kilburn Village Hall

EVENTS PAST

The events below were organised in the past but no longer feature in the calendar of events. Certificates and badges were awarded to successful participants.

CLEVELAND HUNDRED   100 miles

The Cleveland Hundred was organised by the Long Distance Walkers Association on two occasions, 1976 and 1978. Starting from Scarborough the route followed the coast to Saltburn where it turned inland to traverse the Moors taking in Gribdale Gate, Baysdale, Bransdale, Fangdale and the Hambleton Hills to Cold Kirby and on to Helmsley. The final section crossed the Howardian Hills to finish at Malton.
The fastest recorded completions were by Peter Dawes with 24 hours 14 minutes in 1976 and by Roger Baumeister and Brian Harney with 21 hours 16 minutes in 1978.

CAPTAIN COOK MEMORIAL WALK   44 miles

This was staged in 1978 to commemorate the birth of Captain Cook, Yorkshire's famous seaman, 250 years earlier on 27th October 1728. The pilgrimage started from his birthplace at Marton, near Middlesbrough, and finished at Whitby, on the way calling in at many of the places with which he was associated. The next walk should be organised in 2023 to celebrate his 300th anniversary!

NORTH DALESMAN   55 miles

A once only event based on Great Ayton and organised in 1981 to raise funds for the Camphill Village Trust.

SILVER WEDDING WALK   25km

Another unique event which deserves a mention was a leisurely walk over the Howardian Hills organised by John and Norma Mills in 1986 to celebrate their twenty five years of marriage. A reception followed at the Merchant Taylors Hall in York where badges were presented to successful participants.

OTHER PAST EVENTS

A number of events have been organised over the last ten years utilising the routes of challenge walks or long distance paths. These have included the Bilsdale Circuit, the White Rose Walk, the Samaritan Way and the Missing Link.

PROPOSED EVENTS

Hanging Stone Leap 22 miles. Details from Steve Hutchison, 13 Buckingham Drive, Normanby, Cleveland, TS6 0QD.

Out On A Limb 25 miles. Details from R. Chambers, 84 Bournemouth Avenue, Ormesby, Middlesbrough, Cleveland TS3 0NR.

Riveaulx Abbey

PATHS

**A Directory of Official
Long Distance Paths and
Recreational Paths**

Eskdale

miles

Official Paths	Cleveland Way	Moors	98
	Wolds Way	Wolds	80
Recreational Paths	Bounds of Ainsty	Vale of York	44
	Bradley 20	South Humberside	20
	Cleveland Link	Vale of York	44
	Derwent Way	Worlds-Moors	80
	East Riding Heritage Way	Wolds	84
	Beverley 20	Wolds	20
	Hutton Hike	Wolds	23
	Rudston Roam	Wolds	21
	Headland Walk	Coast	20
	Ebor Way	Vale of York	30
	Esk Valley Walk	Moors	30
	Eskdale Way	Moors	82
	Foss Walk	Vale of York	28
	Holderness Way	Wolds	22
	Howden 20	Wolds	20
	Hudson Way	Wolds	10
	Hull Country Way	Humberside	50
	Hull – Hornsea	Humberside	11
	Limestone Walks	Vale of York	50
	Lyke Wake Way	Moors	50
	Minster Way	Wolds	51
	Missing Link	Moors	48
	Newtondale Trail	Moors	20
	Reasty Forest Walk	Moors	16
	Ryedale Round	Moors-Wolds	165
	Scarborough-Whitby Trailway	Moors	20
	Sheriff's Way	Vale of York	27
	Vermuyden Way	South Humberside	20
Links to Adjacent Areas	Coast to Coast Walk	Dales-Lakes	190
	Coast to Coast II	Dales-Lakes	120
	Viking Way	Lincs-Leics	140
	Yoredale Way	Dales	100

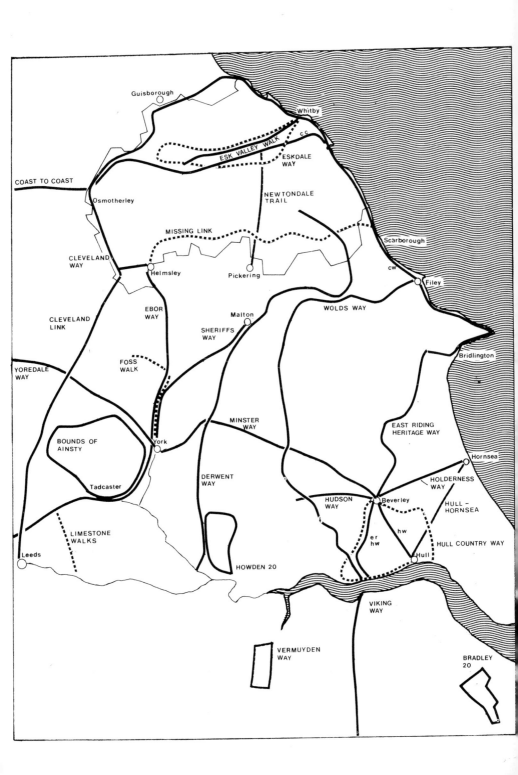

PATHS

Official Long Distance Footpaths
- Officially designated by the countryside commission
- Specific Route
- No time limit
- Route is generally completed in several days of consecutive walking
- Navigational ability is necessary
- Route is waymarked with signposts and acorn symbols except over open country
- Official guide usually available

Recreational Footpaths
- Route instigated by voluntary body, local authority, or individual
- Route is along existing rights of way
- No time limit
- Route is generally completed in several days of consecutive walking, in random sections or, if practical, in one outing
- Published guide or leaflet is available
- Navigational ability is necessary
- Not usually waymarked unless instigated by local authority
- A standard format has been used in displaying information in this section as shown below.

| **BOUNDS OF AINSTY** | Vale of York | **44 miles** |
| name | area | distance |

illustration or badge
(if available)

Tadcaster 484 434 circular
start and finish
O.S. Sheet 105 – 1: 50 000
map   *scale*
No badge or certificate
awards for completion
No Waymarking
path waymarking

Devised by West Riding Ramblers' Association in 1975. The Ainsty is the land lying between the rivers, Nidd, Ouse and Wharfe which was annexed to the city of York in 1449. Lowlevel easy walking

Origin – brief description-characteristics-difficulty of walking

Beating the bounds of the Ainsty, West Riding Ramblers' Association SAE to E.M. Green, 9 Church Avenue, Bilton, Harrogate HG1 4HE.

Where an address is given please enquire initially as to price. No price or postage has been given as these become rapidly outdated. Always enclose a stamped addressed envelope.

Ainsty Bounds Walk Simon Townson, Dalesman Books, 1984

Title of book, author, publisher. Available through booksellers

CLEVELAND WAY   Moors   98 miles

Helmsley 613 838 – Filey 121 819
O S Sheets 93, 94, 99, 100, 101 – 1: 50 000
Badge and Certificate
Waymarked – Acorn Symbols

Opened in 1969 as Britain's second official long distance path. Starting at Helmsley, the path travels three-quarters of the way round the perimeter of the National Park, taking in the Hambleton Hills, the Cleveland Hills and one of the finest stretches of Heritage Coast in the country between Staithes and Scarborough. Few paths capture such a rich variety of walking, scenery and history within such a short distance. A strenuous but highly recommended route.

The Cleveland Way W. Cowley, Dalesman Books 1969
The Cleveland Way A. Falconer, HMSO 1972
A Guide to the Cleveland Way and Missing Link M. Boyes, Constable 1977
A Walker on the Cleveland Way C. Walker, Pendyke 1977
Badge From Lyke Wake Club, Goulton Grange, Swainby, Northallerton, North
 Yorkshire DL6 3HP (SAE)

WOLDS WAY   Moors   98 miles

Hessle Haven 035 256 – Filey 121 819
O S Sheets 106, 100, 101 – 1: 50 000
Badge
Waymarked – Acorn Symbols

Originated in 1968 by The Ramblers' Association, opened in 1982. Meanders along full length of Wolds in a broad arc from the Humber to the North Sea. Heavily cultivated landscape, undulating plains, dry smooth-sided valleys, excellent views over the adjacent vales. Part of the Dales Way – Ebor – Cleveland – Wolds – Viking Way chain of paths stretching some 470 miles from the Lake District to Leicestershire. England's largest natural lake, Windermere, and largest man-made reservoir, Rutland Water, lie at each end of the chain. Moderately demanding walking throughout.

The Wolds Way David Rubenstein, Dalesman Books 1979

The Wolds Way Roger Ratcliffe, HMSO 1982
Wolds Way Companion East Riding RA. Available from Sheila M. Smith
(address below)
Badge From Sheila M. Smith, Wolds Way Recorder, 65 Ormonde Avenue,
 Beverley High Road, Hull HU6 7LT (SAE)

BOUNDS OF AINSTY — Vale of York — 44 miles

Tadcaster 484 434 – Circular
O S Sheet 105 – 1: 50 000
No Badge or Certificate
No Waymarking

Devised by West Riding Ramblers' Association in 1975. The Ainsty is the land lying between the rivers Nidd, Ouse and Wharfe which was annexed to the city of York in 1449. Low-level easy walking.

Beating the Brunds of The Ainsty West Riding Ramblers' Association. SAE to E M Green, 9 Church Avenue, Bilton, Harrogate HG1 4HE.

Ainsty Bounds Walk Simon Townson, Dalesman Books 1984

BRADLEY 20 — Wolds-Lincs — 20 miles

Bradley Wood 240 050 – Circular
O S Sheet 113 – 1: 50 000
No Badge or Certificate
Waymarked

One of the series of recreational paths instigated by Humberside Council. Visits the Lincolnshire Wolds, an officially designated Area of Outstanding Natural Beauty, a green rolling landscape with many attractive villages. Easy walking.

Bradley '20' Recreational Footpath leaflet. From Director of Technical Services, Humberside County Council, County Hall, Beverley, Humberside HU17 0DE.

CLEVELAND LINK — Vale of York — 44 miles

Leeds 334 373 – Kilburn 514 813
O S Sheets 100, 104, 105 – 1: 50 000
No Badge or Certificate
No Waymarking

A low-level route from Leeds to the White Horse at Kilburn where it links with the Cleveland Way which can be followed to the sea at Saltburn. No route description of the Cleveland Way section is included in the booklet.

Leeds to the Sea West Riding Ramblers' Association. SAE to E M Green, 9 Church Avenue, Bilton, Harrogate HG1 4HE.

DERWENT WAY   Wolds-Moors   80 miles

Barmby on the Marsh 690 285 –
Lilla Howe 889 987
O S Sheets 105, 100, 101 – 1: 50 000
No Badge or Certificate
No Waymarking

Follows the river Derwent from its confluence with the Ouse through the Vale of York, Vale of Pickering and Wolds to source on the moors. River, moor, forest, panoramic views, picturesque villages, moderate walking.

The Derwent Way Richard C. Kenchington, Dalesman Books 1978

EAST RIDING HERITAGE WAY   Wolds   84 miles

Hessle 033 255 – Filey 121 809
O S Sheets 106, 107, 101 – 1: 50 000
Badge (also badges for each section)
Waymarked

Pioneered by Glen Hood in conjunction with Humberside County Council to provide an excellent example of what can be achieved by the partnership of the voluntary and public sectors. The route consists of four sections – Beverley 20, Hutton Hike, Rudston Roam, Headland Walk each described below. All are well waymarked in both directions. Each walk has a separate badge, subject to a 12 hour limit, and leaflet. There is another larger badge for those who complete all four routes.

Full details of the routes and badges are available by sending a large 9″ × 6″ SAE to Glen Hood, Shakespeare Junior High School, Preston Road, Greatfield Estate, Hull HU9 5HE. To prevent delays during school holidays send to 329 Kingston Road, Willerby, Hull HU10 6PY. See also pages 12, 13 and 50.

The leaflets for this walk were produced by Humberside County Council and form part of a series of recreational footpath leaflets covering the area. For details send a large SAE to Director of Technical Services, County Hall, Beverley, Humberside HU17 0DE. Tel. (0482) 861291.

| BEVERLEY '20' | Wolds | 20 miles |

Hessle 033 255 Beverley 038 393
O S Sheet 106 – 1: 50 000
Badge Waymarking – B20

Popular walk on the fringe of the Wolds. First section of East Riding Heritage Way.

Beverley '20' and Walks from Skidby Recreational Footpath leaflet, Humberside C.C.

| HUTTON HIKE | Wolds | 23 miles |

Beverley Minster 038 393 Driffield 028 573
O S Sheets 107 – 1: 50 000
Badge Waymarking – HH

Very flat, close to the river Hull, good for naturalists. Second section of East Riding Heritage Way.

Hutton Hike Route Sheet Humberside C.C.

| RUDSTON ROAM | Wolds | 21 miles |

Driffield 028 573 Bridlington 176 680
O S Sheet 101, 107 – 1: 50 000
Badge Waymarking – RR

A village walk, steeped in history. The third section of East Riding Heritage Way.

Rudston Roam Route Sheet Humberside C.C.

| HEADLAND WALK | Wolds | 20 miles |

Bridlington 176 680 Filey 121, 809
O S Sheets 101 – 1: 50 000
Badge Waymarking – HW

The spectacular final section of the East Riding Heritage Way. Includes Flamborough Head Heritage Coast and Bempton Cliffs RSPB reserve.

Flamborough Head Recreational Footpath leaflet, Humberside C.C. and **Headland Walk** Route Sheet.

Glaisdale ▶

EBOR WAY	Vale of York	70 miles

Helmsley 613 838 Ilkley 117 480
O S Sheets 100, 104, 105 – 1: 50 000
Badge and Certificate
Waymarking

Inaugurated 1975. Pioneered by Ken Piggin. Links the Dales Way and Cleveland Way. Low-level, varied walking taking in the beautiful Howardian Hills, the ancient city of York, the Vale of York, Lord Harewood's estate, Otley Chevin and Ilkley Moor. A pleasant, attractive route.

Ebor Way J.K.E. Piggin Dalesman Books 1978
Badge from J.K.E. Piggin, 1 Odeon Buildings, Blossom Street, York YO2 2AJ (SAE)

ESK VALLEY WALK	Moors	30 miles

Esklets 675 016 Whitby 898 115
O S Sheet 94 – 1: 50 000 (extracts in guide)
No Badge or Certificate
Waymarked

Follows the River Esk from its source high on Westerdale Moor to the sea at Whitby in ten short sections. Esk Valley Railway provides return transport. Caters for the family and serious walkers. Excellent walk and guide, mainly low-level easy walking.

The Esk Valley Walk North York Moors National Park 1982

ESKDALE WAY	Moors	82 miles

Whitby 898 108 Circular
O S Sheet 94 – 1: 50 000
No Badge or Certificate
No Waymarking

Embraces a fine stretch of the North York Moors in a circular route which explores both the low-level valley and the adjoining dales and moorlands. A longer, more strenuous alternative to the Esk Valley Walk.

Eskdale Way Louis S. Dale Dalesman Books 1983.

FOSS WALK	Vale of York	28 miles

York 606 510 Easingwold 529 698
O S Sheet 100, 105 – 1: 50 000
No Badge or Certificate
Waymarking

A walk along the river Foss from its confluence with the Ouse at York to Easingwold taking in many interesting waterway features, welcoming pubs and a variety of flora and fauna.

The Foss Walk River Foss Amenity Society, 77 Millfield Lane, Nether Poppleton, York YO2 6NA (SAE)

HOLDERNESS WAY	Wolds	22 miles

Hull 102 314 Hornsea 206 481
O S Sheet 107 – 1: 50 000
Badge
Waymarking

Low-level route, easy walking, explores lesser known rights-of-way in the Hull and Holderness areas. Devised by Roy Dresser of the Hull and Holderness Group of the Ramblers Association. Badges are available only to those taking over 7 hours to complete the walk!

Holderness Way Guide SAE to Roy Dresser, 128 Kirklands Road, Kingston-upon-Hull, Humberside HU5 5AT. Badge also available from this address.

HOWDEN 20	Wolds	20 miles

Howden Minster 748 283 Circular
O S Sheet 106 – 1: 50 000
Badge and Certificate
Waymarking

Devised by Goole and District Rambling Club and launched as a recreational path in conjunction with the County Council. Gentle walking throughout.

Howden 20 Recreational footpath leaflet, Humberside County Council, Director of Technical Services, County Hall, Beverley, Humberside HU17 0DE.

Badge SAE to Mrs Wendy Wales, 29 Mount Pleasant Road, Goole, Humberside DN14 6LH.

HUDSON WAY	Wolds	10 miles

Beverley 877 420 Market Weighton 028 413
O S Sheet 106 – 1: 50 000
No Badge or Certificate
Waymarking

Follows disused railway line, named after the early railway magnet George Hudson.
Hudson Way leaflet, Humberside C.C. – available from Director of Technical Services, County Hall, Beverley, Humberside HU17 0DE.

HULL COUNTRY WAY	Humberside	50 miles

Holy Trinity Church 100 286 Hedon 189 287
OS Sheets 106, 107 – 1: 50 000
Badge
Waymarking

A circuit of Hull devised by the East Yorkshire and Derwent branch of the Ramblers' Association. Moderate walking.
Hull Country Way Recreational Footpath leaflet, Humberside C.C. – available from Director of Technical Services, County Hall, Beverley, Humberside, HU17 0DE.
The Hull Country Way, Lockington Publishing Co., Front Street, Lockington, Driffield, North Humberside YO25 9SH.
Badge SAE to A. Killick, 47 Dene Road, Cottingham, Humberside HU16 5PD.

HULL – HORNSEA	Humberside	11 miles

Hull 110 311 Hornsea 208 479
O S Sheet 107 – 1: 50 000
No Badge or Certificate
No Waymarking

Follows disused railway line across drained farmland. Easy walking.
Hull to Hornsea Information Sheet, Humberside C.C. – available from Director of Technical Services, County Hall, Beverley, Humberside HU17 0DE.

LIMESTONE WALKS	Vale of York	50 miles

Various start points
O S Sheets 105, 104
No Badge or Certificate
Waymarking

A series of four linked walks starting at Wetherby, Aberford, Bramham and Micklefield. Pleasant easy walking in the band of limestone country between Wetherby and Castleford. Includes Lotherton Hall, Bramham Park, Fairburn Ings, Garforth, Ledston Hall and Thorp Arch.
Day Walks in Limestone Country, West Yorkshire M.C.C. Available from Leeds Tourist Information Centre, Central Library, Calverley Street, Leeds LS1 3AB Tel: (0532) 462453

| LYKE WAKE WAY | Moors | 50 miles |

Osmotherley 455 937 Ravenhall Hotel 980 018
N.Y. Moors Leisure Map – West and East
1:25 000
No Badge or Certificate
No Waymarking

An opportunity to complete the Lyke Wake Walk in a more leisurely way, but does not qualify for membership of the L.W.W. Club. Special badge subject to demand.

The Lyke Wake Walk and The Lyke Wake Way, Bill Cowley, Dalesman, 1983.

| MINSTER WAY | Wolds | 51 miles |

Beverley Minster 038 393
York Minster 603 522
O S Sheets 105, 106, 107 – 1: 50 000
Badge
Waymarking

A link between York Minster and Beverley Minster crossing the Yorkshire Wolds and Vale of York using farm, woodland and riverside paths. Gentle walking throughout.

The Minster Way Ray Wallis, Lockington Publishing Co., Front Street, Lockington, Driffield, North Humberside YO25 9SH.

Badge SAE to Ray Willis, 75 Ancaster Avenue, Hull, North Humberside HU5 4QR.

| MISSING LINK | Moors | 48 miles |

Scarborough 026 935 Helmsley 613 838
O S Sheets 100, 101 – 1: 50 000
Badge and Certificate
No Waymarking

Conceived in 1975 by Malcolm Boyes. Links Helmsley the start of the Cleveland Way to the coast at Crookness, north of Scarborough to create a return route. A good variety of walking and scenery. Includes the Forestry Commission's walk from Reasty to Allerton – see page 80.

A Guide to The Cleveland Way and Missing Link M Boyes, Constable 1977.

Badge and Certificate SAE to Malcolm Boyes, 80 Howe Road, Norton, Malton, North Yorkshire YO17 9BL.

NEWTONDALE TRAIL   Moors   20 miles

Pickering 797 842 Grosmont 828 053
O S Sheets 94 and 100 – 1: 50 000
Badge and Certificate

Pioneered by Mike Teanby in 1981. A splendid route contrasting moor, dale and forest as it follows the spectacular ravine of Newtondale. The North York Moors railway offers return transport Easter to October (Tel: Pickering 72508) Varied walking.

Newtondale Trail route sheet from Mike Teanby, Old School House, Village Street, Adwick le Street, Doncaster, DN6 7AD, South Yorkshire.

REASTY BLUE MAN FOREST WALK   Moors   16 miles

Reasty 965 945 Allerston 877 830
O S Sheets 101 – 1: 50 000
Badge
Waymarking – Blue Man

A walk designed by the Forestry Commission to illustrate their work. Includes some good views. Route also forms part of the Missing Link – see page 82.

Reasty to Allerston Forest Walk SAE to District Officer, Forestry Commission, 42 Eastgate, Pickering, Yorkshire.

Badge from Dalby Forest Visitor Centre, Low Dalby, Pickering, North Yorkshire YO18 7LT

RYEDALE ROUND   Moors-Wolds   165 miles

York Minster 603 522 Circular
O S Sheets 100, 101, 105, 106 – 1: 50 000
Badge and Certificate
No Waymarking

An ingenious circuit originated by Ken Piggin taking in The North York Moors, Vale of Pickering, Yorkshire Wolds, Vale of York. Links many of the official and recreational paths in these areas.

Ryedale Round route sheet. SAE to Ken Piggin, 1 Odeon Buildings, Blossom Street, York YO2 2AJ (Callers Welcome)

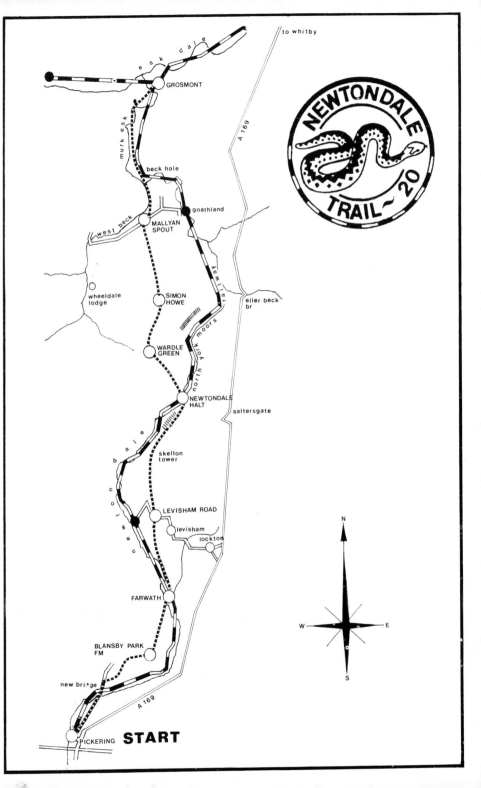

to whitby

GROSMONT

esk dale

murk esk

A 169

NEWTONDALE TRAIL ~ 20

beck hole

west beck

goathland

MALLYAN SPOUT

wheeldale lodge

SIMON HOWE

kem lier

eller beck br

north york moors

WARDLE GREEN

NEWTONDALE HALT

saltersgate

skelton tower

newton dale

LEVISHAM ROAD

levisham

lockton

N

FARWATH

W
E

S

BLANSBY PARK FM

new bri.ge

A 169

PICKERING **START**

SCARBOROUGH AND WHITBY TRAILWAY Moors 20 miles

Scarborough 896 097 Whitby 037 879
North York Moors Leisure Map – 1: 25 000
No Badge or Certificate
No Waymarking

Follows the route of the former Scarborough and Whitby railway opened in 1885. Easy but monotonous walking taking in Scalby, Hayburn Wyke, Ravenscar, Robin Hood's Bay and Hawkser. Good scenery and various railway relics, the most notable being the Esk viaduct near Whitby.

The Scarborough and Whitby Trailway Department of Tourism and Amenities, Londesborough Lane Lodge, Scarborough, North Yorkshire (SAE)

SHERIFF'S WAY   Vale of York   27 miles

York 601 522 Malton 787 714
O S Sheets 100, 105 – 1: 50 000
No Badge or Certificate
No Waymarking

Rowntree Mackintosh Moor and Fell Club launched this walk in 1977. An enjoyable day out through the meadowland of the river Fosse to Sheriff Hutton, then passing through the Howardian Hills to follow the river Derwent to Malton. Moderate walking.

The Sheriff's Way Rowntree Mackintosh Moor and Fell Club. SAE to the Secretary, The Cocoa Works, York YO1 1XY.

VERMUYDEN WAY   South Humberside   20 miles

Haxey 765 999 circular
O S Sheets 112
Badge
Waymarking

Several rights-of-way hve been linked together to form this route named after the Dutchman who drained the Isle of Axholme, so named because it is surrounded by the rivers Trent, Idle, Torn and Don. Easy walking.

Walks South of The Humber Recreational Footpath leaflet, Humberside C.C. – available from Director of Technical Services, County Hall, Beverley, Humberside, HU17 0DE.

LINKS TO
ADJACENT AREAS

COAST TO COAST WALK	Dales-Lakes	190 miles

St Bees Head, Cumbria 960 118
Robin Hood's Bay, N Yorks 953 049
O S Sheets 89, 90, 91, 92, 93, 94, 98, 99 –
1: 50 000
No Badge or Certificate
No Waymarking

Alfred Wainwright, famous for his Pennine Way Companion and Lakeland guidebooks, proposed the idea of a walk across England with the publication of A Coast to Coast Walk in 1972. He encourages walkers to take the initiative and devise their own long distance walks. He has set a classic example. This route stretches for 190 miles; connects three National Parks – The Lake District, Dales and North York Moors; uses existing rights-of-way; and passes over high ground wherever possible. The itinerary includes some of the very best walking in both the North of England and the North York Moors. In the 50 mile traverse of the National Park he takes every opportunity to explore its variety and character to the full. A demanding route for experienced walkers.

Coast to Coast Walk Alfred Wainwright, Westmorland Gazette, 1972.
Coast to Coast Accommodation Guide Available from Doreen Whitehead, East Stonesdale farm, Keld, Richmond, North Yorkshire DL11 6LJ.

COAST TO COAST II	Dales-Lakes	120 miles

Arnside, Cumbria 457 788
Saltburn by the Sea Cleveland 665 215
O S Sheets 93, 97, 98, 99
No Badge or Certificate

A more southerly alternative to Wainwright's going from Morecambe Bay to Osmotherley where it follows the Cleveland Way to Saltburn by the Sea.

A One Week Coast to Coast Walk outline route sheet. SAE to R. French, Wilkin Stile, Bowbiggin, Sedbergh, Cumbria.

VIKING WAY	Lincs-Leics	140 miles

Barton-upon-Humber 032 219
Oakham Leicestershire 862 089
O S Sheets 112, 113, 122, 121, 130, 141 –
1: 50 000
Badge
Waymarked

Links with the Wolds Way which starts from the opposite bank of the Humber at North Ferriby. Leaflets are published by the appropriate local authorities.
Humberside: Director of Technical Services, County Hall, Beverley, Humberside C.C. HU17 0DE.
Lincolnshire: Head of Secretarial and Legal Services, County Offices, Newlands, Lincoln LN1 1YL.
Leicestershire: County Offices, Glenfield, Leicester

Badge and Accommodation Leaflet SAE to Lincoln and South Humberside RA 32 North Parade, Sleaford, Lincolnshire.

YOREDALE WAY	Dales	100 miles

York 600 521 Kirkby Stephen 774 083
O S Sheet 91, 98, 99, 105 – 1: 50 000
Badge and Certificate
No Waymarking

Another route by Ken Piggin, this time following the river Ure, or Yore as it was known in ancient times, from the point where it joins the Ouse north of York, to the high Pennine fells near Kirkby Stephen.

Yoredale Way K.E. Piggin, Dalesman Books 1980

Badge from K.E. Piggin, 1 Odeon Buildings, Blossom Street, York YO2 2AJ.

NOTES

- Safety,
- Sponsored Walks,
- Equipment
- Food,
- Information,
- Accommodation
- The Right to Roam,
- Organisations

Scarborough

SAFETY

1 A sound knowledge and experience of map reading, equipment and safety are necessary under conditions which can induce fatigue and impair judgement.

2 Devise a route schedule taking into account hours of daylight available and check progress against it.

3 In order to eliminate the risk of navigational errors, if possible survey the route beforehand in sections, making notes and taking relevant compass bearings.

4 If you have a support party ensure everyone knows precisely when and where you are to rendezvous. Failure of support parties to locate walkers can lead to rescue teams being needlessly called out. Arrange a central telephone point so that messages can be passed if you decide to retire, or inform the police so that time is not wasted looking for you.

5 Leave word of your route and make sure there are at least three people in your party.

6 Obtain a local weather forecast before setting out and be prepared for the worst: sudden weather changes are common.

7 Note the location of telephone boxes and possible escape routes.

8 The distress signal is six blows of a whistle or six flashes of a torch, both at one minute intervals.

SPONSORED WALKS

1 Sponsored walks in the countryside involving distances over 20 miles have become a popular means of fund raising. As such walks often involve individuals not accustomed to walking long distances it is essential that all aspects of organisation and safety are fully considered. To this end the Ramblers' Association has published a booklet entitled: Sponsored Walks in the Countryside. For details send a stamped addressed envelope to the Ramblers' Association, 1/5 Wandsworth Road, London, SW8 2LJ.

2 Large groups of sponsored walkers have undoubtedly contributed to some of the major erosion problems on the North York Moors. Organisers of such walks are advised to contact the National Park office at Helmsley for recommendations on suitable routes.

EQUIPMENT

1 Checklist for Challenge Walks

* Map and map case
* Compass
* Whistle
* Walk schedule and pencil
* Waterproof jacket and trousers
* Woollen hat
* Food to eat en route
* Drink

* Spare jumper and socks
* Ten pence pieces for telephone
* Torch, spare batteries and bulb
* Emergency rations
* Polythene survival bag
* First-aid kit
* Boots with patterned sole

2 Rules for challenge events specify precisely what is to be worn and carried. These should be strictly adhered to otherwise disqualification will result. In addition to the above items, a mug and the exact contents of the first-aid kit may be specified.

3 Before attempting any of the long strenuous routes in this book it is essential that walkers acquire a sound knowledge of equipment and clothing needs through experience on shorter less demanding outings. It is emphasised that equipment does not have to be costly; fashionable expensive gear does not make a good walker! Shorts, tracksuit bottoms, thermal long johns, waterproof jacket and over-trousers provide a combination that can be adapted to cope with all but the severest winter conditions.

4 Heavy boots with rigid soles and stiff uppers will probably be expensive, take a lot of breaking in and rapidly sap energy. Experienced walkers with strong ankles may find lightweight boots or strong trainers with a deep ripple or studded sole suitable for the North York Moors and Wolds.

REMEMBER LONG DISTANCE WALKING IS GOOD FOR YOU!

FOOD

1   There are no miracle foods or drinks which make the Lyke Wake Walk seem like an afternoon stroll! Practice, inherent ability and long-term bodily adjustment are more important factors in performance.

2   A general rule for eating during demanding walks is little and often so that the body does not become overloaded with the burden of digestion as well as muscular activity.

3   Generally the body is the best guide to immediate food and drink requirements. As muscle activity and sweat loss deplete the body of vital substances, preferences for types of food change. Foods which are readily attractive, palatable and digestable under normal conditions can differ from those required after fatigue has set in. Discovering which foods do or do not suit you is largely a matter of trial and error.

4   It is common knowledge that sweating is not just a matter of water loss. Salt tablets (sodium chloride) are often taken during hot weather to avoid cramp. However, potassium and magnesium are just as important as sodium. Specialist drinks are available which help replace body salts lost in activity. 'Staminade' is a brand popular among some long distance walkers as it is available as a powder which can be mixed with water at convenient stopping points. It also contains glucose to aid energy output. Write for details of local stockists to Nicholas Laboratories Limited, Slough, SL1 4UA.

5   Sweet foods are usually consumed to assist energy output. Glucose is the fastest acting source of energy. The rule of little and often applies particularly to glucose and other forms of sugar, otherwise the body will over-react producing a low blood sugar level which will ultimately leave you feeling more fatigued.

6   A common myth among active people is the need for plenty of protein. Several experiments have shown protein loss during activity to be no greater than when at rest. Eating protein will do nothing to aid performance; indeed, some nutritionists consider high protein intake, especially meat, to be damaging to health.

7   Listed below are some of the more popular foods consumed during demanding walks:

* Rice pudding and tinned fruit
* Jam sandwiches
* Salad sandwiches
* Cake
* Chocolate

* Fresh fruit
* Sweet tea and coffee
* Staminade
* Complan food drink
* Glucose tablets

INFORMATION

Humberside County Council

The Director of Technical Services has assisted in promoting a number of the recreational paths and challenge walks which appear in this book. An excellent range of leaflets has also been prepared to enable the general public to explore and enjoy the local countryside. If you require information or have any complaints about public rights-of-way in Humberside, please contact the Director of Technical Services, Humberside County Council, County Hall, Beverley. Tel: (0482) 867131.

North York Moors National Park

The North York Moors was designated as a National Park in 1952. As such the park authority has the duty of both protecting the exceptional beauty of the landscape and promoting its enjoyment by the public.

Information Centres:

The Moors Centre at Danby is the main visitor centre for the park. Exhibitions, bookshop, souvenirs, tea shop. Open April to October 10am to 5pm. Free admission and parking. Tel: (0287) 60654.

Other tourist information centres:

HELMSLEY	(0439) 70401	SCARBOROUGH	(0723) 372261
HUTTON-LE-HOLE	(07515) 367	SUTTON BANK	(0845) 597426
PICKERING	(0751) 73791	THIRSK	(0845) 22755
WHITBY	(0947) 602674		

Publications:

An extensive range of booklets is published by the National Park Office and includes information on the Cleveland Way and Moorland Safety. The North York Moors Visitor is the official newspaper of the Park including features on different areas, activities and accommodation. All enquiries should be made to the National Park Information Service, The Old Vicarage, Bondgate, Helmsley, North Yorkshire YO6 5BP. Tel: (0439) 70401.

ACCOMMODATION

The Youth Hostel Association provides a network of hostels throughout the region. Write for membership details: YHA National Office, St. Albans, Hertfordshire, AL1 2DY.

Accommodation details are published in the North York Moors Visitor (see above), in the Yorkshire and Humberside Tourist Guide (available through booksellers) and in the bed and breakfast guide of the Ramblers' Association (see page 93).

MOORLAND MUSINGS

Why dost ta' throw thi rubbish here,
Tha mucky lout?
Tha drinks thi beer
And throws t' bottles hereabout:
Tha ates thi grub
And leaves all t' paper lyin' here.
Hest ta' noa gumption?
Man canna scrub
The floors of moors and hill.
Hesta noa sense
With all this towny frills
Mucky lout?

F.A. Rush
The Mute Inglorious, 1930

This walk should not be taken after the 12th August, during the shooting season, without permission from the gamekeeper, Mr Patterson, Wheeldale Lodge, Goathland, and it must be understood that no dog goes for the walk – great care should be exercised on the moorland, so as not to disturb the game, nor endanger the "cheepers" (half grown grouse). It is also respectfully suggested that only strong athletic women accustomed to going on tramping tours should go with their "men-folk" because it is impossible to explore this rugged district without considerable fatigue.

W. Ridley – Makepeace
Walks and Talks on the
North Yorkshire Moors, 1931

THE RIGHT TO ROAM

One of the greatest challenges facing the outdoor movement is gaining the right of access to uncultivated areas of open country. Over a century of campaigning and conflict both in and out of Parliament led to the creation of the National Parks and Access to Countryside Act of 1949. Following on from this, in 1952, the North York Moors was designated a National Park with a governing body, under the 1949 Act, to secure by agreement, compulsory order or acquisition, public access to open country. In 1987, 35 years later, there are still no specific proposals to provide any such areas of access. It is a lesson of the past, in the Peak, Bowland and on Barden Moor that access is not gained without public and political pressure. The Ramblers' Association is currently continuing the struggle for more effective legislation to give the public that general right of access to upland areas which is enjoyed throughout much of Europe. It can only be successful if there is greater public awareness and involvement in these issues.

Open Country: Public Asset or Private Domain, Ramblers' Association, 1982
Make for the Hills, Ramblers' Association, 1983
Freedom to Roam, the struggle for access to Britain's moors and mountains, **Howard Hill,** Moorland Publishing, 1980.

No owner or occupier of uncultivated mountain or moorland shall be entitled to exclude any person from walking or being on such land for the purposes of recreation or scientific or artistic study, or to molest him in so walking or being.

Access to Mountains Bill, 1888

Measures, including legislation where appropriate, shall be introduced to ensure access to open country and water for the purposes of recreation.

European Sport for all Charter
Council of Europe 1976

ORGANISATIONS

Long Distance Walkers Association

The LDWA was founded in 1972 by Alan Blatchford and Chris Steer. Although it encompasses all categories of long distance walking, it caters primarily for those interested in challenge walks. There is now a dedicated following of some four thousand members with local groups in most parts of the country including Cleveland, North, East and West Yorkshire. Several one hundred mile challenge walks have been organised in all parts of the country including two on the North York Moors, in 1976 and 1978. One of the main attractions of membership is the newsletter appropriately called Strider, edited by Chris Steer. A comprehensive calendar of challenge events is included together with general articles and news of local group activities.

For membership details send a stamped addressed envelope to the **LDWA Membership Secretary, Lodgefield Cottage, High Street, Flimwell, East Sussex TN5 7PH.**

Ramblers' Association

The RA has played an important role in the creation of both official long-distance paths and recreational paths. It also works to preserve the footpath network and secure access to open country; conserve our natural heritage against encroachment; oppose harmful legislation; and also helps promote recreational walking.

Membership benefits include receipt of their magazine Rucksack, a comprehensive bed and breakfast guide and details of local walk programmes. Send a large stamped addressed envelope to **The Ramblers' Association, 15 Wandsworth Road, London SW8 2LJ.**

Fell Runners Association

The FRA exists to encourage and foster better standards of fell running and allied mountain racing throughout the United Kingdom. Membership includes the receipt of The Fell Runner magazine and a fell running calendar of events. For details send a stamped addressed envelope to **Membership Secretary, Pete Bland, 34a Kirkland, Kendal, Cumbria.**

British Orienteering Federation

Write for details to **BOF, National Office, Riversdale, Dale Road North, Darley Dale, Matlock, Derbyshirt DE4 2JB.**

Compass Sport magazine incorporates the official magazine of the BOF together with reports on fell running and wayfaring. Send for details to **Ned Paul, 37 Sandycoombe Road, Twickenham, Middlesex TW1 2LR.**

Permanent orienteering courses have been set in the areas below.

Dalby Forest – Pickering Forestry Commission Wayfaring Course. Maps from Dalby Information Centre Enquiries. 0751 60295.

Olivers Mount, Scarborough – Maps from Scarborough Sports Centre, Filey Road. Enquiries 0723 60262

York – Four courses are available in the area. Maps from Eborienteers. Enquiries 0904 769290.

North York Moors Association

Founded in 1985 in order to protect and enhance the characteristic beauty of the North Yorkshire Moors for present and future generations.

Write for details (SAE) to **Dr D. Tilley, 7 The Avenue, Nunthorpe, Middlesbrough, Cleveland TS7 0AA. Telephone enquiries: 0642 316412.**

Camphill Village Trust

In 1939 Dr Karl Koeing opened a school for mentally handicapped on the Camphill Village Estate in Aberdeen. Later in 1955 he acquired Botton from the Macmillan publishing family and established the Camphill Village Trust which now has over seventy centres in seventeen countries. Today Botton Village is highly self-sufficient with several farms, a forestry section, sawmill, creamery, bakery and various workshops. Botton is not an institution and provides people with the opportunity to develop their potential to be useful and productive members of the community.

Visitors are welcome. A coffee bar, gift shop and bookshop are open mornings and afternoons. Telephone enquiries: (0287) 60871. **Botton Village, Nr Danby, Whitby, North Yorkshire, YO21 2NJ.**

North York Moors Railway ▶

INDEX OF WALKS

ACKNOWLEDGEMENTS

Tom Burns for material and photographs on A.J. Brown, Canon Atkinson and Moorland Memorials.

All Walk Secretaries for information and statistics.

Acknowledgement is given to the respective sources from which quotations have been taken:

A.J. Brown, Striding through Yorkshire, Country Life Ltd.
J.B. Priestly, A book of English Essays, Pelican Books.
H.B. Browne, The Story of the East Riding of Yorkshire, A. Browne & Sons Ltd.
A.J. Brown, Moorland Tramping, Country Life Ltd.
William Cobbett, Rural Rides, C.H. Kelly.
H.L. Gee, Good in Everything, Methuen & Co. Ltd. (Samaritan Challenge quotation).
Bill Cowley, Moorland Perspective and Shepherds Round quotation.
Canon Atkinson, Forty Years in a Moorland Parish, Macmillan & Co. Ltd.
F.A. Rush and W. Ridley-Makepeace, Walks and Talks on the North Yorkshire Moors, A. Brown & Sons Ltd.

Photographs:
Cliff Megson, pages 39, 44, 66, 67, 75, 85, 91 and 95
Camphill Press, pages 21, 22 and 36
Tony Marr, page 2
Cleveland Classic organisers, pages 51 and 57
Trevor Robinson, pages 7, 30, 60